SAFETY & SECURITY IN HOTELS AND RESTAURANTS

DR. Raj Kumar Singh
D.H.C.T. Mgmt. (W.B.)
P.G.D.B. Mgmt. (U.P.)
C.F.N. (Delhi)
MHCIMA (London)
Ph.D. (Management)
Director
'SAMS' Institute of Hotel Management,
Varanasi

AMAN PUBLICATIONS
NEW DELHI (INDIA)

Published by
Rajiv Jain for Aman Publications
LG-4A, Ganpati Bhawan,
4675-B/21, Ansari Road,
Darya Ganj, Delhi - 110002
PH: 23255012, 23282127
E-mail: sshjbs@yahoo.com

First Edition 2007
ISBN-81-8204-035-3 (HB)

SOLE DISTRIBUTOR
JINDAL BOOK SERVICES
LG-4A, Ganpati Bhawan,
4675-B/21, Ansari Road,
Darya Ganj, Delhi - 110002

Laser Typesetting by:
S.M. Graphics, Delhi,

Printed by:
Indraprastha Press , Delhi, India

PREFACE

Security has always been a key issue for hoteliers. Hotel security encompasses areas such as security of the property itself, company assets, employees' and customers' personal belongings and valuables, life security, personal security, and job security among others. The events of the past two decades have heightened awareness for proper security and the need for upgrades in equipment, where required. Running a hotel today is a much more complex than ever before. Increased responsibilities and demands on our time, make the job of a hotel owner or general manager a very difficult one.

Hotel security services aims to serve the security needs and interests of customers, employees and the property. It meant to protect the guests and prevent crimes by the application of professional security means and techniques. The security services tries to implement the prescribed security procedures by providing an environment which allows for activities in the facility to continue in an orderly fashion. To accomplish this, security must be fully integrated into the administration as its function is basic to general administration and management so as to provide its protective and preventive activities within the organisation at all times.

Today's lodging security professionals are having a tremendous impact on the reduction of crime in many cities, as well as helping the legal system identify the types of criminal activity within the travel and tourism industry. Given this fact, it is essential that both the public law enforcement agencies and the criminal justice system realise the importance of private security in the lodging industry. The continuous efforts of visionaries in lodging security have had a great impact on how hotel security is perceived by others.

This book gives new and better understanding of every facet of hotel security including the security problems, the role of security, pertinent applications of modern technology to loss prevention techniques and the interdependent relationship that exist between the security and top management. It will be an essential reference for owners, managers, professional security personnel and students of hotel administration.

CONTENTS

Contents

1

INTRODUCTION

Safety and security are often left on the back burner until a crisis occurs. By then, people fall victim to crime, get robbed, get assaulted, become sick or even die. Although we mention "safety and security" in one breath, and despite the interrelationship between them, safety and security represent two different subjects.

SECURITY

Security encompasses areas such as security of the property itself, company assets, employees' and customers' personal belongings and valuables, life security, personal security, and job security, among others. Let us take one "security example" related to employees' personal belongings and valuables in a hotel environment: In all workplaces management stipulates that it is not responsible for valuables and employees personal belongings (their handbags, items kept in the personal lockers, etc.). Yet management must take all possible measures to prevent theft among employees and of employee belongings through its hiring practices and through the implementation of effective management, human resources and operational policies, such as:

— Background checks of selected applicants

— Policies related to employees' entry to, and exit from, the workplace

— Spot checks of locker rooms and lockers

— Effective supervision and control during the work cycle

— Policies related to the discovery of criminal records and wrongdoing among, and by, employees

— Control of people entering and exiting the workplace

With regard to guest valuables, management informs guests that the hotel is not responsible for valuables left in the room, advising them to secure these in safety deposit boxes provided by the hotel. Besides taking care of security issues related to the people they employee, management must undertake some necessary measures, among which:

— Providing "secure" (safety) deposit boxes and areas to keep valuables

— Policies and practices to ensure the security of these boxes and areas

— Management and operational policies regarding the security of guest rooms

— Management and operational policies regarding the security of public areas

— Security policies and practices for the back-of-the-house areas

— Employment and training of security personnel

— Policies and practices to minimise the "presence" and "patronage" of "shady characters" and criminals, verification of registration and check-in personal data and documentation submitted, and curtailing free movement of unknowns on the premises, as well as direct, free flowing communication with local, national and international security authorities)

— Training of staff in guest and valuable security Effective supervision and control procedures.

Safety

It is management's duty to ensure "safety" in several areas, such as:

— The structure itself

— Installations and fixtures (check electrical, plumbing, air-conditioning and other installations)

— Public and work areas (e.g. slippery floors, hazardous obstacles in traffic areas), safety of furniture, equipment, appliances, and utensils.

This is followed by:

— Health safety (nontoxic cleaning material and detergents used)

— Good quality air (what we breathe, dependent upon the type of equipment, installations and fixtures used, and regular repairs and maintenance)

— Food safety (a whole world in itself including sanitation, food quality, food spoilage, correct handling procedures, allowable and recommended temperatures, etc.), and checking and control procedures.

An important "preventive measure" is eliminating the possibility of communicating contagious diseases. Even if local regulations do not require it, it is recommended to send food and beverage handlers for regular medical checkup. Another preventive measure is the formulation and implementation of policies and procedures related to employee accidents which may present a threat to food sanitation. Culinary staff who cut themselves accidentally at work, as often happens while slicing food products, have to immediately stop handling food, and report to their executive chef and to the person in charge of first aid in their company (Security or Human Resources Department) for preliminary treatment and handling.

Healing and precautionary measures are taken before they are allowed back at their job. There are also some basic "dress" requirements for staff involved in food and beverage preparations: e.g. chefs' hats (to prevent hair and whatever hair contains to fall into the food), discreet earrings (non-dangling) or no earrings for women, and long hair neatly and securely tied in a bun at the back of the head.

Of no lesser importance is the safety of work tools and work procedures covering all areas, such as stable ladders, secure shelving, safety shoes, well-fitting work garments, clearly written and complete safety procedures and guidelines from management, safety training, and safety installations and equipment, e.g. fire fighting units, regular maintenance schedules for safety equipment and installations, wider traffic areas (to prevent accidents), adequate staffing, and last but not least, continuous effective training in work procedures. All of this necessitates comprehensive planning, the creation of clear policies and work procedures, organisation, implementation, training of supervisors and employees, supervision and control.

Security Threats in Lodging Industry

Hotel companies that do make the decision to "go global," as well as those already operating offshore, will benefit from addressing a key area of business risk-physical security and other life safety risks arising from various forms of workplace violence and other crime. International expansion mergers, deregulation and privatisation often drive revenue growth, operational efficiencies and benefits to customers. But they can also be breeders of employee discontent, labour unrest, potential criminal disruption and terrorist actions.

Fire safety is also a major area of risk and source of litigation for organisations around the world. Because of these risks, hospitality organisations doing business in foreign markets should avoid the mistake of replicating the management models, construction design, security systems and training programmes that work for them in their home countries.

Just as risk must be carefully assessed in the marketing and financial arenas, hospitality companies also need rigorous risk "audits" when it comes to life safety systems and crisis management. Questions for managers of international operations should include a range of questions.

— How much does our company know about the threats that can arise from criminal activity in regions or countries within which we operate?

— Are our security and life safety processes sufficient given the rise in threats to hotel properties in these destinations?

— Do these systems represent a comprehensive safeguard reflecting the realities of mobility and access to information in today's global community?

— How can we "design in" safety for our workforce and our guests?

Bombings

Most prevalent in all regions. In Africa, for example, there were 182 bombings or attempted bombings between 1990 and 1998, while Asia reportings showed a count of 358. Latin America at 344 and the Middle East at 119. Bombings typically result in extensive property damage, high incidence of injury and lengthy disruption of operations, not only to the target company, but to adjoining businesses extending blocks or miles from the bombing target. In March of last year, for example, Colombian authorities were able to foil a plot by guerrillas to detonate a car bomb at a hotel in Colombia.

The hotel was the site of a major international banking conference, with guest speakers including the presidents of Colombia, Panama and Peru. The apparent motive was to show solidarity with guerrilla groups in Peru. In April 1998, an international chain hotel, located in Uganda, was the target of a bombing resulting in five deaths. India has experienced a number of bombings this year. During October 1997, terrorists attempted to place a truck bomb at a five-star hotel in Colombo, Sri Lanka, but were stopped by hotel security from gaining entrance into the parking lot. The terrorist thereafter parked the vehicle near two other five-star hotels, detonating the device causing major damage to the hotels and surrounding buildings and killing eleven people and wounding 105. The hotels were located near government buildings.

Assaults

The second most frequent offenses reported after bombings. Not included on the earlier table because of the difficulty of capturing total data, assaults take the form of shootings, murder and physical assaults on a person. Various police jurisdictions report high numbers.

Kidnappings

This threat has emerged as a problem worldwide, reaching critical levels in Colombia and Mexico. Kidnappings are conducted by terrorists, criminals and others acting for political reasons. Most of the kidnappings are motivated by economic reasons, but in some cases are undertaken to effect political change in a country. Most are resolved peacefully, but some have tragic results.

Organised Crime

The threat from organised crime elements has reached global proportions. The threat ranges from the well-developed economies of the United States to such places as Hungary, Russia, India, South Africa and other emerging markets. Organised crime groups, sometimes working in concert with distant organisations, are generally engaged in transporting stolen goods internationally, extortion, murder, bombings, drug trafficking, arson and bribery of government officials.

In Hungary, organised crime has been responsible for killing a diplomat, newspaper publisher, the bombing of several political candidates' houses and offices, as well as more than 100 other bombings since 1991. The most brazen was in July of this year, when a car bomb detonated in the centre of the tourist district, killing four and injuring 25 people. The apparent target was the owner of a restaurant and tourist resort.

Corruption

The International Monetary Fund, World Bank and Inter-American Development Bank are all addressing the issue as it relates to projects with which they are involved. The U.S. Commerce Department estimates that companies worldwide operating outside their own national borders, paid approximately $80 billion in illegal payments or bribes to officials in other countries since 1995. For an industry involved in operating buildings, the fact that corruption is extensive in the construction area should be of particular concern to hospitality managers. Where building inspectors are paid to overlook poorly constructed buildings or lack of compliance with building codes, there is a potential for disaster.

Such activity has resulted in a number of incidents, including building collapses resulting in injury and death. Clearly there are risks for hospitality companies "going global," particularly in markets where there is a history of political and economic instability. Hotel organisations frequently rely on security systems that are transplanted from property to property. But hospitality managers should consider a number of pertinent questions.

— When was the last complete security survey completed for all facilities?

— Is the system sufficient to the threats in the local area?

— Have new risks developed since the last surrey?

— Is there an effective emergency management plan in place?

— Will staff be proficient in its execution?

When reviewing threats in a country or region, it is important to focus not only on what directly appears to affect the hospitality industry, but also on the environment as a totality. A detailed security audit, combined with well-designed life-safety systems and training programmes at individual properties, is essential. The following list might be regarded as a minimal risk assessment before venturing into many, if not most, markets outside one's home base of operations. Portions of the checklist also apply to undertaking security audits for hospitality properties planned or in operation in the home country:

Prior to physically launching operations, an analysis should be conducted of the country and of the market within which the hotel is located—whether it be a city or non—urban environment. The risk assessment should encompass the identification of particular criminal problems and crime statistics, as well as the evaluation of local and regional law enforcement agencies. The agency review should in particular focus on an assessment of proficiency, training, degree of professionalism and level of response to incidents.

Special Problems

Prostitution is a problem that, if not controlled, can ruin a hotel's reputation. The word controlled was used intentionally, for prostitution cannot and will not ever be eliminated. The security objective should be to reduce such activity to an absolute minimum. There are a number of simple control methods a hotel can employ. First, guest registration procedures must be established and followed closely. All guests must be required to show valid photo identification such as a driver's licence and preferably a credit card when checking in, even if they are paying cash in advance for their stay. The reason for the tight registration process is that most streetwalkers will not carry identification.

The more sophisticated "call girl" or "escort" type of prostitute will have identification, but she or he also represents less of a threat to the innkeeper. The second method of control can be utilised in properties that have computerised front desk procedures and can print out a complete list of all guests by room as well as list the number of occupants registered in that particular room. Once given that list, particularly at night when guests are returning to their rooms with visitors they may have just met in the local bar, the security officer can screen all incoming guests at the front door. This method has two benefits.

First, the innkeeper is entitled as a matter of law to additional revenue if a second person is staying in the room. Second, if in fact the "visitor" is a streetwalker, not only will he or she not have identification as noted above, but the guest may not want to risk having a second person listed on the registration folio. The final two methods of prevention include employee cooperation. The housekeeping department will know if a certain guest-room has heavy traffic going to and from it and can alert security. Secondly, hotel managers must maintain a no-tolerance attitude toward prostitution while supporting security in its efforts to deal with the problem.

Common meeting places for prostitutes are lobby pay telephones, bars, and easily recognised hotel fixtures such as chairs, plants, and the like. There are two general types of problems associated with bars, restaurants, stores, and the front desk in a hotel. They are check and credit card fraud, and theft of merchandise including food and beverage items. Incidents involving "walk-outs" are common when non-paying customers enjoy a meal and/or drinks in a hotel and then proceed to leave without offering to pay for the items consumed. Unfortunately, this type of crime is only a misdemeanour in most states and innkeepers are very limited in what they can do after the event.

Frequently, if the patron is caught leaving, they can be confronted and—if they refuse to pay—be held long enough for security or the public police to arrive. The thief then can be identified for future reference or prosecution. The amount of the loss usually is not worth the time required to prosecute, so it is recommended that the name and description of the individual be recorded and distributed to all outlets in the hotel. You may try alternate means of payment. If the person tries to obtain food or drink again, they can be refused until they pay for the previous bill.

Credit cards very often are used as a means of payment by patrons because of their convenience and the generation of tax records for business purposes. This convenience, however, has caused some problems for the hotel operator, particularly in food and beverage outlets and stores. The security department must face problems ranging from guests using stolen cards and cards over their allowable limit to dishonest employees inflating gratuities or even writing in gratuities. The best means of avoiding these and other scams is to develop detailed policies and procedures for authorisation of use, and to train employees to follow the procedures. Charging store merchandise to a guest-room, for example, must somehow be verified first.

Management must then follow up to ensure compliance with the rules, and violators should be dealt with appropriately. If security is called to investigate alleged wrongdoing by employees and the allegations are proven, swift and severe disciplinary action should be taken after all levels of disciplinary action are considered. Disciplinary action can range from counselling to termination. The sale and use of illegal drugs are major issues in any industry, but appear more complicated in the lodging industry.

The innkeeper must be concerned not only with employees, but also with guests and patrons who become involved with using and selling drugs. The use of drugs by employees on or off the job presents some serious consequences for both performance and safety. With the cost of workers' compensation insurance rising so high and representing one of the largest line expenses for liability, employers must address the increased use of drugs by employees. Only recently have employers begun to consider the possibility that some employee accidents are directly related to drug use on or off the job.

Even employees who do not use drugs but who are aware of others who do are affected. Morale problems are likely to arise among employees who want to do their job well, but see others not performing because of drug use. Furthermore, a work environment that allows employees to sell drugs to co-workers will create the impression that management does not care or is incompetent. Although still controversial at this stage, employers may wish to consider the possibility of drug testing on employees who either have declining performance levels or who have exhibited unusual behaviour or evidence of drug use.

Legal counsel should be consulted before this action is taken. A number of legislative reforms on intoxication on the job have been enacted recently, including denying benefits in cases in which accidents are alcohol- or drug-related. Talk to legal counsel about your state's legislation. Effective ways to deal with substance abuse problems are complicated. The long-term solution is education and awareness, not policing employees. The hotel should have an Employee Assistance Programme (EAP), which may reduce the incidents and cost of alcoholism and other abuse at work. Yet we must be realistic and acknowledge that both alcoholism and drugs do exist in the lodging industry.

Most hoteliers wait until drug dealing is rampant before they act on tips about drug usage. This does more harm than rapid action because, by the time management reacts to the problem, more employees are involved and affected, which may result in having to remove more staff from the hotel. Security managers also can consider using undercover investigators posing as employees to determine who the dealer and buyers are, as evidence for termination. Drug use or sale by guests is not an unusual problem, but is one that hotel operators should be prepared to resolve.

It is very unlikely that a hotel manager will be able to prevent a guest from using drugs in the privacy of his or her room. If however, the manager becomes aware of such use, action should be taken. Limited use may best be handled by warning the guest that repeated activity will result in removal from the hotel. However, evidence of more serious use may require assistance from the local police. It is common for drug dealers to use large urban hotels to conduct their drug deals, for the size of the hotel usually will ensure their anonymity.

Certainly, no hotel operator wants to see her or his hotel aired on the evening news as a result of a major drug bust. Liaison with local, state, and federal law enforcement agencies is vitally important. Most law enforcement arrests involving drugs occur off property; however, the legal case may be developed around the actual activity that took place while on hotel property. Training all hotel staff about drug activity awareness will assist security in preventing illegal sales, manufacture, or use of drugs on hotel premises.

Depending on the size and location of a hotel, certain types of public figures are likely to stay as guests on occasion. In larger, convention-class hotels, political figures are often in attendance for social events. Public figures, whether they are politicians or people such as rock stars or sports teams, often will draw crowds. These crowds may be admirers, or they may be demonstrators protesting the appearance of the individual. In either instance, security is faced with the difficult task of controlling the crowd while protecting the public figure.

One should not assume that the local police will always take care of or even be aware of these problems. Instead, the security manager should be prepared to work with the authorities in planning for the person's arrival, stay, and departure. Occasionally, hotel security will not receive any advance notice of the person's arrival. However, if your hotel security procedures include how to handle this type of scenario, coordinating this process should not take very long. Generally, though, there will be varying amounts of lead time available before the event. If this time is adequate, detailed planning will avert risk with minimal difficulty.

The hotel may make reasonable regulations governing the conduct of its guests, provided such regulations are applied to all persons, without discrimination. These regulations can be designed to prevent immorality, drunkenness, or any form of wilful misconduct, e.g., loud obnoxious behaviour, drug activity, etc., that may offend other guests, may bring the hotel into disrepute, or may be inconsistent with the generally recognised properties of life. The hotel has the right to evict any guest who wilfully violates these rules. Obviously, the eviction must be done in a reasonable manner. If guests refuse to leave the hotel after their attention has been called to the violation and they have been requested to leave and given a reasonable opportunity to do so, the hotel may forcibly evict them.

The hotel may use only such force as is reasonably necessary to accomplish this goal. Management personnel and security officers should be carefully instructed on this point and the hotel should obtain the assistance of the local police. When a hotel guest becomes ill with a contagious disease, the hotel management, after notifying the guest that she or he must leave, has the right to remove the guest in a careful manner and at an appropriate time to a hospital or other place of safety, provided this does not imperil the guest's life.

As a practical matter, however, it is preferable to consult with an attorney and report these matters to the proper local authorities. Usually the local authorities will take charge and remove the sick guest. The illness of an indigent guest should be reported to the local department of welfare, communicable diseases should be reported to the local health authorities, and psychiatric cases should be reported to the police. Security managers must ensure that they are knowledgeable about many types of crime, with special attention to those that may occur at a hotel—

even if one would normally think they are unlikely to occur.

Confronting the Challenges

The hotel-owner's duty or standard of care is legally defined as taking reasonable care to protect against foreseeable acts. In a suit alleging negligence, the plaintiff must show that the defendant hotel-owner had a duty to use reasonable care to protect the plaintiff or victim from a foreseeable act, that the defendant failed to perform this duty, that this failure was the proximate cause of the incident, and that the plaintiff actually suffered loss or injury. The basic security elements for hotel industry are: deadbolt locks, viewing devices, chain locks, doors and frames, and communication devices.

In some instances, when the risks of crime are known to exist, additional security has been recognised as fundamental under the circumstances. In these cases, courts have often held that the following elements are required as a matter of law: track bars for sliding glass doors, closed circuit television, and security guard personnel. Very often hotel chains have corporate security departments consisting of only a few people. This generally happens not because the company ignores its security needs, but because the security employees are assigned as staff to various corporate facilities.

So while dozens or even hundreds of people may have a full-time or part-time security function, the corporate staff is limited. Each facility staff member should have a specifically assigned role to play in the security programme. From housekeeping and maintenance to front desk and executive management staff, everyone should be trained and encouraged to participate in security programmes.

Special areas that require total participation of the staff include: general disorders and bomb threats, fire emergencies, overall surveillance, first aid response, maintenance checks, parking lot patrols, response to calls for assistance, record keeping, eyewitness testimony, and internal security. Whether security personnel are employees of the facility or are provided under a contract with a security service, or even if they are part-time off-duty law enforcement officers, among the things to be considered are the following:

— All personnel should have a copy of, and be familiar with, the security manual.

— All personnel should undergo a competent training programme emphasising those subjects that deal with the institution's security needs.

— All personnel should be readily identifiable as security officers if they are to have public contract.

— All personnel should be issued and trained in the use of appropriate equipment.

— All personnel should be regularly supervised and evaluated with a record maintained of their performance.

— All personnel should undergo a background evaluation, which can reveal suitability for employment in a hotel.

— Contract security personnel should be employed under a contract that sets specific duties and responsibilities for which they can be held accountable.

— All personnel should possess a licence necessary for their employment and for the possession and use of weapons and equipment.

— All personnel should receive regular and updated training and testing on their skills and knowledge to their employment.

Thoughtful analysis should be given to the manner in which law enforcement officers are employed. Different regulations of the country govern the employment of police personnel in private security assignments. In addition, civil liberty issues and conflict of interest possibilities may also be considered in the decision to utilise off-duty police. Decisions on these issues should be made with the advice of the counsel. The hotel should employ any technology it acquires to its full capacity. The reason for this is, that by purchasing it, the hotel is both acknowledging the need for the system, and advising the guests that they are under the protection of the equipment in place.

In the event of loss or injury, that might have been prevented if the installed equipment had been working to its full capacity, the hotel-owner has more claim to defend against. Close circuit television can be an effective security tool when installed and used properly. It should be placed in areas with the greatest likelihood of effective use. Generally remote areas, such as parking lots need coverage, because other eyes and ears are not available for security purposes. Electronic door locks are useful to gain better control over room access problems.

Maintaining adequate key control has long been a vexing problem. Mini-safes have become useful because theft from guest-rooms are responsible for the greatest percentage of reported hotel-related crimes. Maintaining adequate insurance against claims of negligent security is essential both to defend against claims and to pay damages if awarded.

Not utilising an investment in security equipment can be as bad or worse than not making the investment at all. The development of a clearly defined procedural manual is the backbone of the security programme. The procedures manual not only directs the security effort, but also serves as evidence that security considerations have been carefully and logically thought out.

Good lighting is an important crime deterrent and prevention tool. In an environment of increasing all-round crime, increased crime in hotel-related matters is not a matter of surprise. Hotels in particular are looked at as targets for local criminals, who see a fertile source of victims carrying cash and valuables. It is common to find criminal elements from adjacent neighbourhoods or those who are even willing to travel relatively long distances for the promise of a good haul from unsuspecting victims.

Certain categories of guests require special security consideration because of behaviour-patterns, special needs, cultural differences or other characteristics that cause security problems to develop. These individuals and groups require special attention to ensure that their stays do not result in preventable losses or injuries to themselves or others. Foreign visitors are often victimised by criminals because they are tricked or misled into placing trust in dangerous individuals or bad advice.

Convention guests or large groups are frequently targeted by burglars, prostitutes and con artists because of the ease of penetrating the group and learning about patterns of movement and conduct. Convention groups should receive special reminders about security hazards, should be encouraged to practise stringent requirements concerning the use of deadbolts, chains and peepholes, and encouraged to cooperate with overall hotel rules and security personnel.

Women travelling on business now represent 40 per cent of business travellers. These women often travelling alone, and have in recent years become the victims of especially brutal crimes including assault, rape and murder. Care should be given with room assignments, and every effort should be made to place women on notice of foreseeable risks. Airline flight crews, and particularly female members of these crews, have been identified by criminals as targets because the regular patterns of their stay is so easy to identify.

Room thefts and personal assaults are higher than average for these crews. Student groups, especially those attending proms or other school functions, often lack adequate supervision to ensure that they conform to rules and procedures. Trade shows, especially catering to industries involved in valuables such as jewellery, furs and electronics, attract thieves from all over the world. Group tours, because of their scheduled departures and the practice of leaving luggage and purchase in lobbies, storage rooms and unattended guest-rooms, suffer a high incidence of loss.

Celebrity guests, especially entertainment groups or sports teams, regularly suffer attempts by fans, curious, and persons with criminal intent, to accost them in public spaces, on sidewalks around the hotel, and even in their rooms. Always make reservations ahead of time and secure them with your credit card. Otherwise, if area facilities are overcrowded, you may find yourself stranded in unfamiliar surroundings or in an unsafe room. If your room is not ready, ask to store your luggage in a locked room. Many hotels have a "dry room" where you can put your luggage and freshen up.

If the hotel has more than one building, request a room in or near the main building. Request a room that faces inward towards other rooms or towards the lobby. Request a room that does not have easy access to the window, such as from the roof or street. Request a room on the second floor, but not higher than the seventh floor, near a fire exit, away from stairwells, elevators, ice machines, basements or garbage/refuse rooms. A room near the elevator helps avoid long walks down stairways.

If you have valuables or important documents, e.g., passport or airline ticket, store them in the safety deposit box at the front office and get a receipt. Use a room safe to store only items of moderate value. Large sums of jewellery or money should be placed in the safe at the front desk. If there is no room safe, put valuables in a money belt that you may wear, or bring along a "portable safe". These come in many forms: hollow books, shows with hollow heels, suitcases with hollow compartments, etc. Always use the deadbolt lock when in your room. Always use the chain lock which should be securely fastened to the wall and a solid core door.

Windows should open and close easily from the inside. Use the extra lock or stick on windows, sliding or patio doors so that they do not lift out of their tracks. If someone comes to the door, use the peep hole and ask the visitor to identify himself/herself. Call the front desk to confirm the identity of the visitors, even if they reply they are with room service, janitorial, etc. If you are expecting someone, pre-arrange an exact time of arrival, as well as some form of introduction or identification: a secret knock, business card under the door, or a phone call from the lobby.

Completely close the curtains, especially in the evening or if you will be away from the room for sometime. Public announcements are a means to disseminate information about terrorist threats and other relatively short-term and/or transnational conditions posing significant risks to the security of American travellers. They are made any time there is a perceived threat and usually have Americans as a particular target group. In the past, public announcements have been issued to deal with short-term coups, bomb threats to airlines, violence by terrorists and anniversary dates of specific terrorist events.

Importance of Physical Security Survey

Once the in-country and market area assessments are complete, the next step is a physical security survey. If done thoroughly at the outset, it may reduce the frequency of need for future assessments. Terrorism, for example, is currently a dominant concern in some environments, but the emphasis can shift quickly if the subject property becomes the target of guest room theft or assaults. The common link here, however, is perimeter security and access control. Both of these issues should be addressed in the physical security survey.

Such a review would not only consider the physical issues such as perimeter security and access control, but also the likely origins of the threat whether it be terrorist, criminal or labour related. The survey should include the identification of vulnerabilities and critical operational components, such as communications, power supply and valuable storage and data processing areas. Furthermore, it should encompass assessment of access control points, perimeter security, alarms/CCTV, lighting and finally a detailed review of security procedures.

Crime-Prevention Design

New construction should include a crime-prevention design audit. Design for crime prevention in hotel development can he highly beneficial. To be considered are such factors as the relationship of buildings to parking areas and structures, lighting, perimeter views and protection, and security systems.

Role of Safety and Security Committee

Effective management of safety and security is made possible only by appointing an overall safety and security coordinator (preferably a department head) who will form a safety and security committee, composed of a variety of department heads and assistant departments, with himself/herself in the role of safety and security committee secretary. Such centralisation will enable effectiveness and efficiency of the committee, bringing up the subjects for discussion and follow-up on implementation.

Usually, the chief engineer and the scurity manager of the organisation are co-chairs of this committee. The safety and security committee must conform and cooperate with national, state and local regulations, submitting reports to the authorities where required. Committee members establish policies, procedures and training strategies, to cover all areas related to safety and security, including "Emergency Procedures" (e.g. accidents, fire control, assault, robbery, mad acts by employees, visitors or guests, and all other possible cases which would present an emergency). They delegate responsibilities to different department heads, departments, and specific employees.

They communicate to the organisation at large and implement widespread training, including drills and simulations. Hotel Managers usually have clearly written instructions to guests for cases of emergency or fire, informing them of what action to take, e.g. (a) call the operator or (b) Leave your room, take the nearest staircase (emergency exit) and do not use elevators in case of fire. They affix a clear map with instructions on the inside panel of guest room doors. Bellmen, who help with check-in, explain and show emergency exits to newly arrived guests.

The safety and security committee is the most important one in an operation since well-being and lives are at stake. Meetings are held at least once a month, while the appointed subcommittees who take "field action" meet oftener. Meetings regarding safety and security are not intended for the exchange of idle banter. Their duty is to ensure safety and security of the property and all the people who are in the property.

Each member comes with a ready-made agenda for discussion and has to report on experiences and observations. Minutes of the meeting should be clearly written and distributed within two days at the utmost. The safety and security coordinator follows up on decisions taken at the meetings to ensure immediate action and ensures effective training material, strategies and activities.

Pre-Employment Screening

All hotel employees should have a thorough background check conducted. There have been a number of instances in which hotels have hired individuals with criminal records in illegal drug sales or theft. Incidents of drug dealing, time-clock tampering and guest theft are relatively common problems that can be greatly mitigated with thorough employment and criminal checks. This process is especially important when selecting security personnel.

Employee Training

These programmes should be developed to enhance security among all hotel staff, in addition to the security force. Employee training should not only include a focus on hotel functions (guest relations, check-in procedures, daily operations, and administrative responsibilities) but security awareness as well. As is the case at most hotels the security staff is limited and is sometimes strained due to commitments and shrinking staff. By providing the entire hotel staff with training in the identification of security issues, a description of operational methods, where to report information and periodic updates on security advisories. Management can in effect add additional "eyes" and ears to the organisation.

Security Planning

It is important to broaden the focus of risk and systematise processes. Each hotel, for example, should have a detailed bomb threat plan that covers procedures to include:

1) the reporting person;
2) execution of the search plan;
3) what to do if a suspect package is found; and
4) evacuation plans.

The process is critical because time is always of the essence. Many bomb threats are made for the purpose of disrupting a company's operations. Needless evacuation of a facility can play into the hands of the person making the threat. On the other hand, information must be properly handled because of the scope of the potential damage.

2

Structure and Functions of Lodging Security Departments

Most hotels and motels are concerned with security and have measures in place to prevent crimes against patrons. At the same time, however, hotels and motels continue to be targeted by criminal elements. Security in the lodging environment presents a wide range of challenges if only because the lodging business is in operation every hour of the day, every day of the year. Inexpensive safeguards can usually be implemented at a budget motel, but the more significant and costly safeguards tend to be put on the back burner.

Unfortunately, it is the absence of the significant safeguards that leads to litigation. On the one hand, budget motel management may recognise the need to upgrade security and appreciate the attendant liability risk, but on the other hand, may lack the financial resources to do anything about it. Even with new construction or retrofitting for expansion or other non-security purposes, management may be unable to find enough capital to fund needed security improvements. With the exception of safe deposit boxes at the front desk, which limit a motel's exposure to property loss, no codes or laws require a motel to provide physical security.

Courts across the nation have mandated that motels must merely take "reasonable" precautions to protect their guests from physical harm. The public has become more educated concerning personal safety. In an overbuilt lodging market with heavy competition and fewer people travelling, hotel and motel owners are responding to their customers' concerns about personal safety.

Six very fundamental security steps that involve time but little cost can be implemented at the budget motel:

— Managing by walking around (MBWA) involves getting into the trenches and seeing what's going on in the business, and getting close to customers and employees. The really small "Mom and Pop" motels practiced MBWA before Tom Peters put a label on the concept. The larger, multi-unit motel chains are often lacking in this valuable practice. MBWA is a caring attitude that is imparted to employees and guests alike. Many security professionals emphasise having a written policy and programme, and although written materials can be helpful, they cannot engender the caring attitude and genuine concern that must be projected for security to succeed.

— A background investigation that includes contacting prior employers and making criminal records checks should be conducted before employees are hired. This is the second step. This is important because applicants may falsify prior employment information in order to conceal personal defects that make them unsuitable for assignment to high-trust jobs. The value of background checking is apparent at the budget motel where only one or two employees are present in the evening hours. At stake are the care and custody of the motel and its assets, and the protection of the patrons and their valuables. These are awesome responsibilities that cannot be placed into the hands of people about whom little is known.

— Employees need to be involved in security. One way to promote involvement is to make employees aware of security risks, how the risks affect the motel, the staff and the patrons, and what the staff can do to offset risks. The American Hotel & Motel Association offers a series of training video workshops on the basics of lodging security. Workshops cover everything from awareness to handling disturbances. Another consideration is to motivate employees to carry out their security responsibilities, especially with respect to emergency response procedures. Programmes that provide rewards, such as a deserved thank-you from a supervisor, a certificate of appreciation, recognition by co-workers, a day off or a merit bonus, can go a long way to building a security programme. It is not unusual in the lodging industry for an employer to pay for performance as opposed to paying for time spent on the job. The quality and quantity of work, especially work that is central and essential to the business, is recognised as having a higher value than hours spent at the workplace. Incentive programmes can include financial rewards for excellence in security.

— Having a liaison with local law enforcement is crucial to the small property operator. Without adequate police protection, the budget motel is at extreme risk. The property management can contact the local crime prevention unit to identify the criminal threats confronting the motel and to learn what the police and the management can do to improve security at the property. At a minimum, the local management needs to know the nature of the police services that are available, the manner in which those services are performed, and the officers who deliver the services.

— The motel manager needs to communicate with neighbours. The idea is to share information about crime in the neighbourhood and to look out for each other's interests with respect to spotting and reporting suspicious activity. Neighbours can also share details of their successes and failures in setting up countermeasures to local crime. These are the kinds of activities that defend against allegations that the motel management was negligent by not recognising crime risks that can impact its patrons and by not having a security programme at least equal to that of nearby competitors.

— Patrolling of the premises should be done during the hours of darkness and whenever crime presents a threat to property or people. Patrolling can be handled on a proprietary basis by designating in-house employees to perform the patrol (as full-time or add-on duties) or patrolling services can be handled on a contract basis with a security guard company.

Unlike other security specialists, the lodging security manager operates in an environment where the protected group is nearly always changing. With the exception of the employees working on the property, the guest population changes nearly everyday. A wide spectrum of society is represented in the guest population; also represented are the problems the guests bring with them. As with any facility security programme, the security manager will develop a loss prevention plan and programme based on the results of a survey. Ideally, although seldom the case, the survey will occur prior to the facility being constructed.

The survey of a hotel is similar to that of a survey for any other facility, except possibly that more attention must be paid to the surrounding area. The foreseeability of crimes is a concept that has great significance at lodging facilities, requiring careful analysis and formulation of effective countermeasures. Lodging operators have been placed on notice by the courts that the owner/operator "may be liable for failure to warn guests and to prevent criminal assault where prior criminal activity in the area should have made the attack on the hotel guest foreseeable to the owner/ operator". Lodging industry professionals are clearly faced with a duty to act to protect guests. The security survey is an element in meeting the duty.

STRUCTURE OF SECURITY DEPARTMENTS

The structure, size, and reporting level of a security department will differ widely by hotel chain or company, due to the fact that there are presently no standards of organisational structure for certain size hotels. However, these factors will affect a department's efficiency and success within a hotel. A typical department structure consists of the security manager, assistant manager, shift supervisors, and security officers. The structure ideally coincides with the size of the property, which usually is categorised by the number of rooms. In most hotels the department head usually will be called the director or manager.

Commonly, the title "Director of Security" is used to denote multiple property responsibility or multi-job function responsibility. He or she reports to a member of senior management—either an operations manager (resident manager) or directly to the managing director (general manager). A "Security Manager", on the other hand, is usually responsible for a single property, or else has the primary job function of security and reports to varied levels of management depending on the company. It is very important for the department head to have an assistant who can substitute when the manager is not present and manage the department operationally on a daily basis.

A security department will encounter difficulties operating effectively with just a single person in charge.

There will always be some situation to which the department head cannot attend, due to the usual limitations of a regular work schedule. A hotel cannot afford to depend on the availability of a single individual. The role of the assistant security manager should be just that—to assist the director/manager by shared job tasks such as scheduling, payroll, training, hiring and firing, and coordinating department meetings.

The assistant in most hotels must be capable of working flexible hours and days. The management structure of a security department should include shift supervisors: individuals designated as being responsible for the officers working a given shift. The supervisor is the vital link between employees and security management. The supervisor represents management's needs and views to the officers and at the same time has the responsibility of representing the needs and views of the officers to management. Without a knowledgeable supervisor available, the staff are left to make decisions in haphazard ways.

A lack of structure could lead to an increase in poor decisions. Even if there are no actual supervisory personnel, some system of supervision must be in place. Little instruction material is available concerning the individual lodging security employee's role, contribution, or importance in the overall security function. It must be remembered that regardless of how knowledgeable security management may be, the line employee's performance is the ultimate measurement of success.

The security officer's daily patrolling and presence have a deterrent and prevention effect that must be acknowledged. This is true both for employees and would-be criminals intending to commit a crime. The size of a security staff required will generally be proportional not only to the number of rooms, but also to size of the facility and the number of employees on the hotel payroll.

It also will depend on a number of factors that must all be considered simultaneously.

In a pre-existing hotel, it is somewhat easier to determine staffing needs by reviewing the history of problems and guest-related issues addressed by security. If there are records available for review, a workload analysis can be conducted to indicate the types of calls for service and their distribution according to times and days of the week. One rule of thumb that deserves mention concerns the number of staff required to cover a single post around the clock, for three eight-hour shifts. The number is not 3, but 4½ or 5 persons, to allow for days off, vacation, sick time, training and other administrative tasks. Other important factors to be considered include the design of the property and the location of the property relative to both the neighbourhood and the type of setting.

An urban hotel in a high crime district should anticipate overflow problems from the neighbourhood, such as streetwalkers, vagrants, and trespassers. A hotel in a suburban location that is accessed only by motor vehicles and is surrounded by a residential community is less likely to experience the problems of the urban property. Crime rates, economic growth or decline, climate conditions, and the availability of public safety resources such as police, fire, and ambulance services must all be taken into account when planning staff size and distribution. The level in an organisation to which security reports will greatly affect the ability of the department to achieve desired results.

Lodging security departments have been known to report to a wide variety of managers, including the managing director, general manager, operations manager, human resources manager, building superintendent, and—perhaps most commonly—the rooms division manager. Ideally, however, the security department should report to the highest level as possible; the operations manager is practical, for example. If the property is operated in such a way that the general manager is accessible to the security manager, then this is the person to whom security should report. A general manager's schedule is often so busy that it precludes regular accessibility except to a few senior managers.

The security manager needs to be able to communicate routinely with the senior manager who oversees the security department. Some security professionals lack a broad company-wide perspective on the role of security. Their narrow view does not take into consideration how the entire operation is affected by their department. Security solutions must be consistent with the overall operation of the hotel. Closing the general storeroom at night, for example, may reduce losses in inventory, but such a "loss prevention" decision will also have an adverse effect on other departments such as banquet and F & B (food and beverages) personnel who need items immediately.

Functions of Security Personnel

The most basic function for the security personnel in any hotel is to perform regular patrols of the property, both inside and outside. There are three different types of security patrolling that have been utilised in hotels for decades, yet continue to serve the needs of guests, employees, and the property in general: random routine patrol, lobby patrol, and basic rounds. In random routine patrol, the security officer walks, or in some cases drives, around the property on a random basis to check for irregularities, suspicious circumstances, and intruders.

There are two objectives achieved by this type of patrol. First, any irregularity or suspicious circumstance hopefully will be discovered before a major problem develops. The second form of security patrol commonly employed in a hotel is lobby duty or surveillance. Any area of the hotel open to the general public requires a different type of patrol. The officer who is assigned to a public area, such as the lobby, must stay in one general location for extended periods of time to fulfil his or her duty. There are three benefits or purposes filled by this type of security presence: observance of undesirable persons or behaviour; assisting guests or others; and, deterring crime as a visible presence.

The third and most traditional form of security patrol is the fire watch. It differs from randomised patrol, although both may be accomplished simultaneously. On a fire watch, the officer patrols every floor and section of the building, including locked areas, in hopes of discovering any potential fire hazard, smoke, or actual fire. It is a common practice to utilise some type of watch clock, checklists, or an electronic wand to record what items or areas were checked and at what time.

Caution should be taken by security managers to control the keys and discs that are imprinted from this equipment to prevent tampering and destruction. Accurate records should be maintained with the daily log books and incident reports, mostly for insurance purposes but for legal purposes also. A contemporary version of the watch clock is an electronic device that reads barcodes similar to those used in grocery stores.

The officer carries the device, which is about the size of a hand-held calculator, and passes it by a code placed on a tag at the location to be checked. At the end of the shift, the officer can insert the device into a recorder, which will read all rounds made, critical areas missed, and so on, and generate a hardcopy printout. Any of these measures is helpful to enhance the level of watchfulness necessary during late night hours. An important aspect of patrolling for all security personnel is the awareness of arson signs.

Arsonists are known to use hotels as avenues for committing theft by setting fire to one location and, while everyone evacuates, stealing the guests' or hotel's property. Other arsonists like to watch people evacuate from buildings and will usually blend in with the crowd watching the scene. The typical arsonist has little concern for a facility's occupants or the firefighting personnel. Arsonists, particularly a professional "torch", will use flammable liquid in quantity. Look for liquid containers that may hold accelerants that can turn a small fire into a major fire in a short time.

One accelerant of which most people are unaware is the basic corrugated cardboard; it will burn intensely. Other items to be noted and acted upon include: dynamite charges connected with primer cord; hydrants or sprinkler valves that have been shut down or have deliberately damaged threads to prevent hose hook-ups; and unusual odours such as gasoline, kerosene, or fuel oil.

Documentation is essential to the proper operation of a security department in any environment. Reports usually generated by a hotel security department include incident reports, activity or shift reports, and safety rules violations. Well-written, typed, and accurate record keeping is very important and helpful to the future planning of the hotel in general and of security specifically. A security manager should be able to review the previous year or more of reports and identify patterns of activity that will help direct available resources in the security programme. Security reports are important as records for insurance or prosecution purposes; they should be thought of as important management tools, not locked away in a storage room or discarded.

It is easier to maintain and research incident reports if they are kept chronologically. Caution should be used when storing these records; a fire file safe is recommended. Be sure to check the state statute of limitations for civil action suits and keep all records for the required time, as well as keeping records for specific pending cases until the cases are completely settled; check with your legal department. Hotels offer a wide variety of services to guests, and like most other businesses they also maintain a lost-and- found department.

The number of found items a hotel can accumulate varies with the size of the hotel and the volume of business within the hotel. Property that is turned in to security can potentially belong to a guest, patron, employee, or someone passing by the hotel. For ethical reasons as well as ensuring that all found property is secure, all lost-and- found items should be turned in to the security department daily. The property should be logged in and only given to its rightful owner on request. Lost-and-found sheets are critical, as well as a lost-and-found log book tracking the property chronologically.

Security in Casino Industry

The casino industry is growing larger as each day passes and is being associated with hotels. Security managers fortunate enough to work with either the hotel side or the casino side at hotel chains need to ensure that they are familiar with gaming regulations and related laws. It is important to realise that there are various types of casinos that have emerged with the proliferation of legal gaming. Casinos are being developed in historic or refurbished structures, and river boats are being used to operate as floating casinos or moored casinos. There are also casinos in purpose-built facilities, which may have limited non-gaming amenities.

With gambling, there has been a trend toward allowing people to have greater control over their choice of activities and to be more responsible for the consequences of their own actions. But this principle has not been applied uniformly over the so-called "vices" such as alcohol, tobacco, illicit drug use, prostitution, and pornography. These vices have economic and social impacts on the hotel and/or casino similar to the impacts of gambling. The likelihood of these vices being introduced into the casino is very high.

Security managers should study their local gambling and lottery ordinances to find out what is and is not allowed. In addition, they should check with their local public prosecutor to find out what cases he or she is willing to act on and how the courts interpret gambling statutes. It is a known fact that the gamblers as well as persons who attempt to conduct scams are all well-versed in gambling laws. Don't be surprised to find people who attempt to challenge casino games, testing the parameters in order to commit acts which may be on the legal borderline.

Likewise, don't be afraid to ask for help from a gaming investigator in identifying marginal cases. Emerging casino security practices, using CCTV equipment, call for gaming machines and tables to be individually identified with a location mark and casino logo. The identification, coupled with video recordings, allows taped incidents to be admitted as evidence in gaming commission hearings as well as in court. The casino security strategy is people-watching, which is nothing new. Employee theft is not new, either, especially when millions of dollars pass through the hands of employees each day. As visitors and employees come up with new ways to cheat, many eyes should be watching.

The most effective deterrent is people watching people, with most watchers out of sight. Hundreds of cameras can be hidden inside domes or behind ceiling panels. Pan/tilt capabilities, colour monitors, and strategic placement all contribute to cover every square foot of a casino floor. It is important for security staff to study what they see on those cameras to determine if angles should be changed, people should be followed, or if a zoom shot should be taken of a pile of chips. Most states allow tapes from casino crimes to be admissible as court evidence.

Crowding is a problem, due to the fact that river boat designers cram as many gaming positions onto each boat as possible, to take advantage of the enormous revenues generated from each position. One advantage to river boat owners is the fact that the boat is cruising—therefore, passengers do not have the option of leaving and frequently gamble more than they normally would. To alleviate the risks associated with congested spaces, security needs to be involved in the floor planning stage of construction to ensure that foot traffic patterns and passenger movement have been considered.

Another concern is that air circulation is poor in crowded spaces, and smoke-filled air can become an irritant, leading to a less-than-optimal gaming experience for many guests. Surveillance is very important in casino security environments, where criminals range from casino dealers and employees to "railbirds" who steal chips from the sides of tables while patrons are not paying attention. Surveillance specialists look for targets of theft where the stakes are high.

Crimes take place in areas of intense action, where more chips are being played or the value of the game is high. Surveillance specialists also look out for known troublemakers and have a central supervisor or pit boss for every ten tables. Usually, the staff working in surveillance security have worked in hotel security and are knowledgeable enough about guests' traits and mannerisms to assist them in identifying problem people. Another issue for casino security is that the budget needs are far greater than most security departments' needs, due to the vast amount of technology necessary to conduct professional surveillance operations.

Storage of video equipment is an important factor because tapes must be retained in case they are needed for prosecution of criminals or other legal matters. Par stock of replacement equipment also is critical to ensure immediate replacement of any piece of the technology that breaks down. Most surveillance specialists are concerned about having updated and timely identification of known criminals, along with their method of operation. Knowing about these techniques is crucial to casino security professionals and will keep them keen on typical tricks of the trade. One way in which the surveillance specialist can be made aware of these criminals and their methods is through networking systems set up in cities with casinos to share information about incidents that occur at various sites. This networking system can communicate by fax, telephone, or other methods.

The relationship and coordination between the specialist operating the surveillance equipment and the security officer on the casino floor is also crucial. Casino security and hotel security, as professions, need to be recognised as excellent career paths that offer upward movement. These positions develop special talents that should be rewarded accordingly. Both education and experience must be continuous and security professionals must be allowed to grow with the industry. Hotel chains that have surveillance experts need to allow them to assist the industry as it grows by sharing information, training, knowledge, because it is not a competitive area.

Hotel Security Force

Protection officers, particularly at a fixed access point but also to some extent while on patrol, are expected to influence pedestrian as well as vehicular traffic on and around the property. The patrol function includes either scheduled or unscheduled patrol of the perimeter, the grounds area, parking lots, access points and the exteriors/ interiors of buildings. Of particular concern, since the guest is the principal asset, should be patrolling in areas where guests are most likely to be in need of protection—guest-room areas, commonly used walkways and access points, and recreational areas. The escort function touches on protection of the guest, the employees, and other assets.

Escorts might be scheduled or unscheduled. The escort function may be carried out by walking with the person to be escorted, or by supplying a vehicle, patrol car, bus, or golf cart. The inspection function along with the emergency responses function is broader than the other three. We expect protection officers to inspect both on a random and scheduled basis, and further to inspect both "people" and "things". Instances of inspection might include: fire inspections, safety inspections, and security inspections. This, of course, is only a partial list of the many possible inspection duties a manager may expect from his protection officers.

Security officers are traditionally thought of as the first on-property resource to call when emergencies arise. The list of possible emergencies security officer can be trained to respond includes: medical emergencies, fire emergencies, weather emergencies; and criminal emergencies. There is additionally a sixth function to which some protection officers are assigned, and that is a training function. Sophisticated security departments have sometimes been given the additional task of training and such duties might include training in: CPR/Heimlich manoeuvre, first aid, fire extinguisher usage, safety programmes, and self-protection. It should be stressed that protection officers, when properly selected, trained, equipped, managed and empowered, can become the most effective of all countermeasures available.

During civil liability cases, juries require reasonable care, with or without protection departments or officers. Testimony which shows that the staff itself affected such care can be as influential as the existence of a protection department. If indeed, a staff is so trained, then protection officers may not be the countermeasure of choice. If a lodging manager, after the analytic review of possible protection needs, opts to establish a protection (security) force, then the same degree of management attention must go into this organisational exercise that would be expected in any departmental development.

Once the need for a protection department is established, it should be placed on the organisational chart at a level equal to other functions. This department should report to the same level to which its sister departments report, ideally to the GM, and it should carry equal weight with those other departments. Nearly as common as the lodging manager's propensity to "pass off" this function to an outside agency or relegate it to inferior status within existing departments is the typical decision making matter when selecting a protection manager. The relegation of the protection function to a minor role within an already existing department such as engineering is usually a mistake.

Selection Procedure of Security Force

The size of the force if often the first question which arises in the mind of lodging management. This is unfortunate and suggests that the value added and return-on investment aspects of the force are secondary to the cost of the force.

The number of guards required normally depends on a careful analysis of the guard expectations regarding the five basic functions which you now know to be control, patrol, escort, inspection, emergency response, and training. The protection manager needs to return again and carefully analysis each of the six functions in terms of the needs and requirements of his property.

— Will the control function be required and if so, how often, how widespread, and for what period of time?
— Will the patrol function be required and if so how often, how widespread, and for what scheduled or unscheduled activities?
— Will the escort function be required and if so how often, to what areas both on and off the property, and will vehicles be required or appropriate?
— Will the inspection function be required and if so, how often, and to what degree?
— Will the emergency response function be required and if so, to what extent?
— Will the training function be required and if so, to what extent?

If this seems difficult and beyond the normal experience of a new protection manager, he might ask himself if there is indeed much difference between this organisational management exercise and one which would be expected in, say, manning the newly conceived F&B function. The characteristics—personal, professional, social—which surround the ideal guard are perhaps no different than those which any ideal employee should exhibit. Some considerations should be viewed, however, when considering employing protection officers. There is no more important trait unequivocally required by a protection officer than that of honesty and reliability. He must be, above all, absolutely above reproach in his personal character attributes.

Depending on the particular tasks to which he is assigned, other character traits come, vitally, into play. He should be well disciplined and both able and adept when interfacing with other people and events in various types of situations. Some situations may be dangerous, some stressful, many difficult. His character should be such that he can adapt to these changing and challenging circumstances and represent the property well in all roles. A protection manager can readily observe that the type labour pool from which protection officers have, in the past, been picked is not particularly encouraging. Even more alarming are these portrayals when one remembers that these employees hold the key to the vault.

There are several considerations and options present themselves to management insofar as "the look" of the force is concerned: uniforms and equipment, communications, arms, and gender. There is no hard and fast rule regarding how or whether to uniform and equip the protection force. Possibilities range from no uniform whatsoever to a rigid police-like look complete with rank and insignia and the attendant equipment trappings. The decision, of course, should be made consistent with the ways this countermeasure is to be used and in what arena. Most properties have opted for a middle-of-the road look—neither totally casual nor militarily rigid.

Typically, the protection officer in contemporary settings will be dressed, consistent with the season and weather and duty location, with a blazer, slacks, neckwear and with optional items including bad-weather gear, boots, and topcoat or a heavy jacket. Equipment requirements will, of course, vary from property to property and from assignment to assignment, but the issue of a flashlight and communications equipment is virtually a given. It is difficult to overemphasis the importance of management having the ability to communicate with protection officers on-duty and on-post and, in turn, providing them with the same ability. The nature of emergencies is such that the ability to communicate and thereby respond quickly and effectively is paramount.

Protections officers, obviously, cannot be at all places at all times. When emergencies arise, they must be dispatched quickly and efficiently. Further, protection officers themselves often encounter emergencies and the need to call for assistance is great. Only an effective communication system can address these needs. In a fixed-post assignment, telephones are normally adequate. However, when a protection officer is on patrol or on surveillance duty or elsewhere when telephones are inappropriate, quick and reliable communication must be available.

While in some uncommon cases one-way communications are all that is required, a pager system may be adequate. More often, however, two-way communications are not only desirable but necessary and such a system should be utilised. Technology is changing virtually on a daily basis so the prudent protection department manager will carefully examine and weigh his options before this usually considerable investment is made. The best universal advice from virtually every expert in this field is when a circumstance seems so fraught with danger as to seem to require the introduction of firearms, then management should take one of two paths: either cancel/adjust the circumstances or, if this is impracticable, use only off-duty police officers as an armed component.

There are three categories of protection officers in hotels:

— *Contract personnel services*: Contract personnel services are available in virtually all areas in which lodging properties exist. These services are offered by firms which specialise in the recruiting, hiring, training, and supervising of guards and subsequently contracting with entities such as hotels to supply that entity with these persons.

Commonly perceived advantages are:

- — less expensive than either of the other two categories;
- — less training time required; less administrative time required (HR files, etc.);
- — easily available replacements;
- — less danger of disadvantageous relationships with staff; and
- — less property liability.

And main disadvantages are:

- — less physical or intellectually qualified than other categories;
- — present less of a professional image;
- — less interested in loyalty to the property;
- — higher turn over resulting in unstable protection force; and
- — likely to be disregarded because of "Rent-A-Cop" image.

— *Proprietary services*: Many properties prefer to develop their own in-house proprietary protection force. Properties, usually through their protection department manager, typically recruit through established classified means, interview, screen, hire and train just as they would any other property department employee.

Commonly perceived advantages are:

- — better quality "handpicked" employees;
- — better training potential;
- — less turnover;
- — more chance of loyalty to property;
- — higher potential for confidentiality and trustworthiness.

And commonly perceived disadvantages are:

- — more potential for undesirable collusion with staff;
- — likelihood of job "stagnation" or boredom;
- — high liability exposure;
- — more training required; more supervision required; and
- — more administrative support required.

— *Off-duty police officers*: In many, perhaps most, police jurisdictions, police officers commonly are available to "moonlight" and make themselves available for part-time employment. Serving as a protection officer is a common choice.

Commonly perceived advantages are:

- — exceptionally well trained;
- — provides on-site a sworn law enforcement capability;
- — can be employed with and is obviously trained in weapons; and
- — presents a strong image.

And commonly perceived disadvantages are:

- — often extremely expensive;
- — presents an unwanted image to staff and guests;
- — potential for being called to other police duty without notice;
- — difficult to manage; and
- — have an enforcement (reactive) mind set rather than one of prevention (proactive).

The selection, training, and supervision, then, of the selected force must meet that goal regardless of the type of guard utilised. If the protection manager decides to staff with contract guards, he must avoid the temptation to also contract the "responsibility" and decision making to that contract agency. Even if a contract agency is hired as the entire protection guard force even including supervisors and managers, the property retains the ultimate responsibility for guest protection and reasonable care.

Such responsibility cannot be delegated; to attempt to do so only results in more complicated liability exposure and increases the likelihood that threats and exposures will develop about which senior management is unaware. It follows then that someone on staff must be designated as responsible for this phase of guest protection and reasonable care. That person must understand and be intimately familiar with the entire scope of the department. He and he alone must be held accountable for the conduct of the department—the decision, the aims, the thrust. Such accountability is essentially to ensure a proper protection level.

The protection manager should not allow himself to be lulled into accepting specifically what the firm has to offer just simply because it is offered. Guard selection/assignment is strange but all too true that protection managers often accept virtually, without question, the guards who are assigned to them. This is but another example of "passing off" the protection responsibility and should never occur. On the contrary, guards who are presented initially to the protection manager should be considered applicants. They should be interviewed, tested, critiqued, and judged just as if they were applicants for any sensitive position. If they meet the protection manager's criterion, they may be brought onboard. If however (and this happens time and time again considering the limited labour pool from which they were chosen) they fail to meet the standards the protection manager has established, they should be returned to the contract firm and replacements demanded.

The protection manager should refer back to his basics which were discussed earlier regarding the various functions he expects the guards to perform. It is very probable that regardless of the level and type training which the contract guard brings to the job, the protection manager will decide that his property's protection needs are such that significant additional training is required. He cannot expect or even hope that the basic training the guard has received at his parent firm is anywhere near the level of, or specific to, what he wants the guards on his property to have. Pre-assignment training, often required in the lodging industry and more often than not conducted prior to being assigned, include such subjects and concerns as:

— specific lodging protection duties;

— specific property rules;

— physical aspects of the property;

— existing safety, security and firefighting procedures;

— location and proper operation of all fire and emergency equipment;

— emergency response expectations;

— areas or subjects of greatest concern;

— locations and proper operation of emergency,

— electrical and HVAC control panels and switches, fuse boxes, steam valves, and hydrants; and,

— locations and proper operation of valves controlling water supply to the fire suppression system.

Training Programmes for Security Employees

Every security department—regardless of the lodging facility size, number of employees, or even number of security staff, for that matter—must have some form of training. Training programmes for security employees fall into two separate categories: a programme for newly hired staff, and regularly scheduled training or ongoing training for staff.

From a potential liability perspective, it is essential to train all security employees before they handle calls on their own and, further, to ensure that the training programme reflects the actual job. In most facilities, training will be tailored around management concerns. Well thought-out programmes will reduce the risk of inadequate training and can be an important aspect of strategic security planning. Inadequate training has been a major downfall of lodging security for years. This is also an area that receives the most criticism whenever legal issues arise about an incident.

Inadequate training claims are based upon either spending an insufficient amount of time on a topic and/ or not addressing issues that will be encountered on the job. For example, if a security officer routinely receives calls for medical assistance, it would be unreasonable not to provide some training in basic first aid. The need for improved training is higher now than ever because the pressure from the public (guests and patrons) has been compounded with the recent recognition of crime rates.

Most people today in any profession are measured by the amount of education and training they have received, which qualifies them to perform their job. For lodging security professionals, both proficiency and success are based on experience and training. Keeping abreast of the current lodging security issues is another important factor. The recommendations of the task force on private security included: a minimum of eight hours of formal reassignment training, and a minimum of thirty-two hours of basic training within three months of assignment.

A maximum of sixteen hours of this time can be supervised on-the-job training. The benefits of a well-rounded training programme will be measured in the security department personnel's enthusiastic attitude and performance, improved morale, and increased incentive to do quality work. One key factor to keep in mind when training personnel is that, to retain quality personnel and assist them in their career development programme, the training must be continuous. Training provides an opportunity for advancement as well as a better understanding of a required task and its importance.

A fire inspection checklist, for example, ensures fire code compliance as well as confidence in one's staff. A security manager could remind his or her staff that if it hadn't been for them ensuring that an extinguisher was operational, a major disaster could have occurred. One of the biggest fallacies made by lodging industry management is assuming that persons coming from another security field or law enforcement need not be trained. Once again, all lodging security professionals should receive training, which should only vary according to the job function of that person within the organisation.

For example, the person filling the position of investigator will have special training requirements that the security officer may not receive. One critical subject usually neglected in training is documentation. Each and every course or programme used should be documented in a file with a copy of the lesson plan, handouts, and other materials; a class roster recording who attended; a copy of the blank exam and each individual's completed exam; and a copy of the certificate issued to each person.

The original certificate goes to the employee, one copy is entered in the employee's human resources file, and one copy is maintained in the security training file. All lodging security personnel should receive the same initial orientation and policy handbook as every other employee. Then, when the security staff members arrive in their departments, the training programme is outlined in respect to their positions.

Security managers are responsible for planning, controlling, and organising a department; hiring and firing personnel; and, ultimately, developing and implementing the department training programme. It is only when a security manager has been given guidance by senior management regarding their philosophy of the hotel that the basic training can be developed expressing policy and procedure for that facility. It is likewise important for the training requirements to be presented in a professional manner that encourages security personnel to be cheerful, cooperative, and tolerant in their dealings within the company as employees.

There are two essential traits for a security manager: good listening skills and patience. If security managers are patient, tactful, professional, and knowledgeable, their employees will learn to respect them and will be willing to seek their assistance. When other employees can trust security, they will be more apt to cooperate in the security function that is vital to both the hotel's and the security department's success. The security manager's attitude about training and its importance sets the climate for the department. A manager who is aggressive and structures the training programme to keep the security staff moving forward and progressing upward will get support from both senior management and the security staff.

3

Hotel Protection Management

Hotel protection management is one of the most important factors in the lodging industry, one must learn to integrate guest protection techniques and practices into the normal management approaches. The guests expect protection; the courts have decreed that we must provide protection; we cannot survive unless we do provide protection. However, a major question among those forward-thinking hoteliers who recognise the requirement to provide guest protection has not been whether to provide such care but how to provide it. We strive to be the perfect host. By word, act, appearance, and design we attempt to send the message to our patrons that they are, indeed, like guests in our homes. We strive to provide easy and friendly access to our properties. How can we succeed at that and at the same time limit or deny access to those we wish to exclude? We design our rooms to be comfortable, inviting and attractive. Isn't it a seeming contradiction to transpose such a welcoming room into one which is bedecked with locks, safety devices and protection equipment? How can we present the friendly, open and inviting atmosphere which the perfect host portrays?

Hotel protection management consists of an integrated management model and series of approaches which, when properly applied, allow for the establishment and maintenance of an acceptable level of protection. And at the same time the image of hospitality is maintained.

Major steps involved in the development of the hotel protection model are the following:

— Identifying and evaluating assets which must be protected.
— Identifying and evaluating the threats which exist to those assets.
— Employing a series of countermeasures designed to minimise those threats.
— Developing a protection profile system from the above listed property-unique aspects and applying accepted management-science techniques thereto.

The term security can be a problem in and of itself, and its usefulness as the term to define protection may have run its course. The term causes a mis-focus and should not be used in a modern proactive, management-science-based property protection programme. There are several reasons for this assertion, not the least of which is the fact that the term security conjures visions of a security officer, private police or a security department. The responsibility of guest protection is limited to those security individuals and security departments, and worse yet, that such care is their exclusive responsibility. This perception is both invalid and dangerous.

Management is art of managing, directing, facilitating or ascertaining the successful accomplishment of tasks or the attainment of stated objectives. In its simplest form management can best be described as that discipline designed and used to get tasks accomplished. This simple definition denigrates the fact that much of today's modern management theory is steeped in and has been developed from theories which were initially university-based. From the early university psychologist/educators, the science of management has been strongly influenced by academic.

From McGregor's Theory X, Theory Y to behavioural sciences and quantitative approaches, virtually all management approaches have their roots in the university setting. The lodging management student should not consider his undergraduate or graduate studies complete without a thorough investigation of various management theories and approaches. A model hotel manager's tools are the same tools every manager has to some degree. They are called the "M" tools and they are the tools he uses to accomplish tasks.

The four "Ms" represent Money, Methods, Machinery and Manpower. To one extent or another, these are the tools which every manager has as he strives to accomplish his objectives. He learns to influence and motivate and make most productive his "Manpower" tools and leads. He learns to develop, adjust and maintain ways and means of getting tasks done reasonably by his tool labelled "Methods". He learns to understand and utilise mechanical and electrical technology which has been developed over the years and his "Machinery" tools come into play. He learns to make the best use of his fiscal resources, and for how to spend and invest and budget them most efficiently his "Money" tools are used. Each of the four "M" tools, individually utilised and manipulated in concert with the other three, provides the manager with the ability to become effective.

This approach, when properly applied, not only protects the guests but significantly reduces costs, increases staff morale and facilitates enhanced property-wide departmental management. It also describes how to change the face of security. In the minds of most hoteliers, security conjures visions of a cigar-smoking, perhaps overweight, retired police officer whose career has been one of reacting to a call. It is designed to change that image to one of a proactive, property-wide management programme which can provide virtual certainty of reasonable care.

Establishment of Hotel Protection Management

The lodging industry cannot hope to achieve the level of guest protection which the courts have imposed upon it without having viable, proven concepts and tools upon which to build a systemised, successful, and legally defendable programme for guest protection throughout the property. Such tools must be workable and easily manipulated to conform to each property's individual requirements. While the term security does not support or lend itself to such a property-wide process, the term protection certainly does. We will begin to examine the proactive aspects of hotel protection management. Both theoretical and practical in the beginning, our focus will be on the tools, concepts, and models of guest protection as they interact with one another and are integrated into overall property management.

Development of Four-phased Approach

The underpinnings of our entire approach to the provision of guest protection is constituted mainly by four phases. Built on the basic canon that guest protection is an absolute requirement, they are the following:

— Phase I Identifying and examining the assets which the Innkeeper must protect

— Phase II Identifying and examining threat to which these assets are exposed

— Phase III Developing countermeasures which minimise the threats

— Phase IV Integrating the resulting guest-protection profile into the entire property-management scheme

This four-phased approach helped the developments of an effective programme of guest protection which, once implemented, will allow the hotelier the comfort of knowing that it is in place and ongoing. This theory and practice termed protection management is not limited to the lodging industry. On the contrary, the four-phased approach to protection works well in virtually any industry group.

Phase I: In any high-tech manufacturing and production facility, assets which require protection will most certainly include the products, proprietary production processes, highly confidential technological research-and-development procedures, and of course, the buildings, equipment, furnishings, and that all-important, highly trained, virtually irreplaceable assets, the employees. When visualising this protection approach, it is important to realise that these assets, collectively and individually, are unique to this facility. They differ in importance, in priority, in scope, and in description from the assets of any other facility.

Phase II: In any high-tech facility and considering the assets, one would consider that threats to those assets would include product theft, industrial espionage, fire exposure to the buildings, and accidents or crimes against persons. It is absolutely vital that one remember that when identifying these threats, they are as unique to this location as the assets are.

Phase III: Once the assets and threats to them have been identified, the manager must embark on the process of identifying those particular, individually selected countermeasures, which are specifically designed to minimise the specifically identified threats to which those specifically identified assets are exposed.

Phase IV: The manager must then integrate his specifically selected countermeasures into his overall property-management scheme, and establish accepted management-science umbrellas over them. He will then assign responsibility demand accountability, and establish training and continuity. At this point, the lodging manager can be said to have begun the establishment of protection management.

Yet there are several major real-world problems which present themselves when such an all-encompassing approach to management is attempted. The important points to be noted are given below.

— Managers often have a built-in bias against security. They find it uncomfortable to accept and difficult to deal with. Of course, they often fear the issue of expense.

— Managers often have difficulty in accepting security on the same management terms and at the same management level as other functional management endeavours such as sales, production, transportation, housekeeping, etc.

— Managers often fail to realise that such protection must be property-wide and property-specific.

All of these dispositions manifest themselves when the lodging manager is faced with the challenge of guest protection. He is burdened with outdated thinking and the short-sighted and limiting usage of what is known as security. He has been too long exposed to traditional thinking which holds to the mind set which leads him to consider protection only after a crime has occurred. And because of outmoded thinking, what is the solution most often considered when reacting to a protection problem? If it ever worked, that state approach was weak at best, and it is woefully inadequate and counterproductive today. It is inadequate because it is reactive.

It is counterproductive because random countermeasure selection either invariably will bring about too much protection. Selection of particular countermeasures must come only after a systematic and thorough analysis of the first two considerations or phases, which are: (i) the assets which need protection, and (ii) the threats against which those assets must be protected. Each property is unique, it follows that the protection scheme designed to protect such an entity against threats which also are unique to the property, must be unique. This individuality must be taken into consideration long before plans are formulated as to what types of protection to apply. Different cities, different neighbourhoods within the same cities, even different locations within the same neighbourhood have different threats. Different styles of building construction invite different threats.

Different construction, different furnishings and different employees all impact to produce different threats. For example, the high-tech plant would require a different protection profile if it were located in a high-crime, urban slum area, as opposed to the exact duplicate facility located in a low-crime, low population, well-protected rural setting. Guests are as unique both individually and collectively as are hotelier's properties, and as such, require unique protection. For example, if a property caters to a young, high-energy clientele, then it is obvious that the protection profile we seek must differ from that which we would establish if the clientele consisted primarily of senior citizens.

We might well pay attention to proper liquor-serving training in the former, and pay more attention to slip-and-fall protection in the latter. To expand this example, consider ingredients of a protection programme we would establish if the property concentrated on business travel versus the protection profile we would expect in a property catering to weekend vacation stays. Then the uniqueness of both the assets and the threats (the guests, in this instance, and the exposures they face), it follows that only after an analysis of both should the means of protection be decided. This approach is facilitated by an extremely useful protection-management model. It is called a Protection Management Matrix.

Basic Assets in Hotel Industry

The three main assets within the lodging industry to be protected are

i) the guest;

ii) the employee; and

iii) physical assets of the property.

Guest

The guest enters the hotel with some expectations, and the ability to meet those expectations is directly related both to his subsequent decision to return and to the hotelier's ultimate success. One prime expectation with which he comes is protection. The guest expects protection. He deserves protection. And the courts have held time and time again that he has a right to protection, and hoteliers are charged with providing it. Every knowledgeable hotelier should know how absolute and critical such vital protection must be. All other considerations, literally, must come only after protection of the guest is addressed.

Employee

The lodging industry's second most important asset is the employee. The obligation to protect employees is steeped in a different set of legalities from those which come into play when we consider protection for guests. In addition to civil courts, here requirements dictate reasonable care for the guest, we are guided and directed with regard to employees by federal and state health and safety laws, along with such dictates as anti-discrimination and anti-harassment statutes, to name but a few.

Physical assets of the property

It is the asset for which the hoteliers is responsible, and

toward which he must direct protection, is actually a collection of assets—the physical, hard, valuable items which are vital to our continued success. They include the property structures guest-room and office contents, vehicles, monies, food and beverage, supplies, etc. While there may be great monetary value represented by these physical assets, they rank only a distant third in the pecking order of assets to be protected.

Major Challenges

The major challenges within the lodging industry are

— fire,

— accident and injuries,

— natural disaster and crime.

Fire: The lodging industry has enjoyed a reasonable and sometimes exemplary history of combating fire. While the tragedy of spectacular hotel fires splashes across the headlines, statistically speaking such occurrences are not common. We are blessed with strong fire codes and easily accessible resources. It causes devastating loss of life, the misery and pain, the terrible financial, professional and personal losses.

Accidents and injuries: The threat of accidents and injuries constitutes the potential for extreme personal and financial loss. They are serious threats and can be significantly diminished through the diligent application of hotel protection management approaches.

Natural disaster: Natural disaster is the prime example that justifies the premise that in hotel protection management planning, universal security standards are suspect and that each property protection plan must be individualised and unique unto itself. The professional protection practitioners insist that standards of protection are needed and long overdue for the entire lodging industry. Natural disaster are most of difficult to deter. The protection management aim with regard to treating this threat, unlike the other three threats, is not proactive. By necessity, it must be reactive, although the planning, as all other planning, must be before the fact. Such protection plans must call for identification of the natural disasters which are possible, or likely, in our own particular geographic area. It is then necessary to plan for the possibility and likelihood of their occurrence, and prepare staffs in appropriate responses.

Crime: Crime is the threat which hoteliers, fear most. Crime can be equally disastrous as fire. It is all-encompassing, terrifying, life-threatening and totally devastating. It can strike with silent suddenness while the remaining occupants of the property are totally unaware. Despite all the attention and research on the subject, it is fair to say that we know all too little about it. The basic and overriding reason for this is we do not know what the root cause of crime is, if indeed one exists. One political faction in the society holds that crime, with all its growth, is a result of a criminal justice system which fails to deliver swift, sure, and severe penalties for having committed crime. The perpetrator of the crime of room burglary will have, obviously, a motive. Usually, it is financial—steal something of value that can be turned into cash. Perhaps to satisfy a drug habit. Or because of illness in his family. Then again, he may simply be greedy or lazy, and decide that his basic living needs are best fulfilled by committing this crime.

To combat crime, the hotelier has no control over motive. There is nothing he can do about ability. Opportunity is the one aspect with which we can be expected to afford reasonable care toward the protection of guests from crime. Remove the opportunity, and you eliminate the crime. Eliminating opportunity is a prime focus of hotel protection management. If yours has a unique exposure to the opportunity of crime, as hotelier, you must develop a unique method of protection against it. Diametrically opposed is the strong vocal, political viewpoint which holds that crime is fostered by that same criminal justice system which is too severe.

And rather than placing convicted criminals into overcrowded, crime-breeding prisons, society should be investing in rehabilitation. Then there are those who argue that education is the answer to crime, and it is the lack thereof which causes crime. The solution to the crime problem eludes us despite claims of politicians at every level, that their crime bill will magically rescue the populace from the grip and fear of crime. We as a society have not discovered a single root cause for crime and therefore it can be effectively argued that without knowing the causes of crime to the extent that we know the causes of fire, the causes of accidents and the causes of severe weather, we are unable to develop a certain cure or prevention for crime. As hotelier, it is essential to remember that not only must we protect guests from crime, but remember too, that little or no help is forthcoming from tax-based resources.

Given the community, the county, the state, and the national police resources, why must we as hoteliers bear the burden of crime prevention on our properties? The answer is possibly a shocker to some, and heresy to others. It is that police know no more than the rest of us, about the causes of crime. Police do respond. They do investigate, interrogate, and all those other good things. They do their best, often under the worst of conditions, to address crime—but only after it has been committed. Innkeepers, on the other hand, must address crime operatively.

If crime is to be deterred and reduced, no one including the police is equipped or budgeted for crime prevention, it falls on us to accomplish the task. Crime is not preventable, it seems incongruous to present an entire section on crime prevention. There is considerable evidence to back up this assertion. Despite studies, research, massive funding and education, it appears that society cannot broadly, prevent crime.

Protection from Crime

That leaves it as the single threat with which the hotelier must deal alone and independently, essentially without any public assistance. Given society's apparent inability to address this threat, this monumental task would seem to be beyond the realm of the hotelier's ability. They can, and in fact, do what society apparently has been unable or unwilling to do. By following specific models, practices and guidelines, he can affect a major impact on that societal menace as it falls within their purview. There are eight countermeasures against crime, the use of which will allow the hotelier to accomplish his obligation to protect the guest.

The selection, application and maintenance of those eight countermeasures are economically feasible, as well as operationally feasible after the property has been appropriately surveyed by the hotelier. These eight countermeasures are in place and being addressed can be assured by the adoption and use of a management model which we call the protection management matrix. This device will serve as a tool for the accomplishment of hotel protection management. Guest protection often has been a subject which the hotelier traditionally has mismanaged or failed to manage. It is a subject with which he has been traditionally uncomfortable. Addressing those discomforts and fears, we can reduce to a total of eight the seemingly endless possible approaches.

Protection is neither steeped in some magical mystique nor is it difficult to achieve. On the contrary, as are all functions within the lodging industry, it is a discipline which can and must be learned, applied, and successful. Our challenge, then, is to confront, head on, the issue of preventing specific crimes to our number one asset, our guests. Our next step in accomplishing this task is understanding the eight countermeasures which can be placed in our protection management matrix. These countermeasures include:

— *Pre-employment verification*: Tradition might hold that pre-employment verification is a function exclusive to human resources, and not something with which an hotelier should be concerned as a guest-protection technique. However, it may be the single most important, most effective, and least expensive countermeasure technique available to the hotelier for provision of guest protection and reasonable care. It has been estimated with reliability and replication that at least 85 per cent of protection incidents that occur on a given property, involve employees.

  This may shock and dismay the reader but it is a condition about which every lodging industry employee should be cognizant. It is a sad truth which the lodging business shares with several other industries. When properly introduced, applied and maintained, pre-employment techniques can and do facilitate extraordinary results. They reduce turnover significantly. They result in vastly improved staff morale. They decrease, astoundingly, the incidents of crime on the property. They act as effective, demonstrable, and impressive evidence of reasonable care if and when litigation is brought against the property alleging inadequate guest protection.

— *Staff-wide training*: The inclusion, as a countermeasure, of such an apparently non-security-related subject as staff-wide training may raise as many eyebrows as did the inclusion of pre-employment verification. There is, however, no more effective and no more all encompassing effort possible across the depth and breadth of the property than the training of the entire staff in the techniques of guest protection. Guest protection and reasonable care training in literally every department are essential. Training must be conducted upon initial hiring. It must be well constructed and documented, and it must continue throughout the tenure of the employee.

— *Access control*: Access control has not been historically isolated, identified and managed as a single protection entity. By definition, access control is that countermeasure which permits, denies, limits, controls or monitors pedestrian and vehicular traffic on, into and out of the property. It can be a significant countermeasure which reduces the likelihood of crime occurring to the guest as well as to the employee. It comes in several forms, designs and applications, depending upon the construction, location and design of the property to be protected. It often begins, depending upon the property configuration, at the perimeter. On many properties, it consists of fencing, shrubbery or other physical constraints.

At the perimeter of the property, as well as along building perimeters, it is most often and most effectively used with the companion countermeasure of lighting. Moving from the perimeter toward the centralised portions of the property, access control begins to take a multitude of forms. It may consist of signs, which direct both pedestrians and vehicles to move, or act, or be restrained in a manner consistent with the wishes of the hotelier. Examples include speed-limit signs, limited-admittance signs, guest-assistance signs, i.e., restroom locations and signs announcing hazardous warnings.

— *Lighting*: Lighting is a countermeasure which is by no means unique to the lodging industry. It has been in use perhaps as long as man has attempted to counteract crime. Further, crime is not the only threat against which man has historically used lighting. He used it in the form of fire, for instance, to frighten away dangerous animals. It is, simply, a countermeasure which works-even against the dangerous, two-legged animals which lurk on and around our properties today. The significant baseline ingredients of lighting are: placement, focus and intensity. Management challenges for the lighting countermeasure to crime are highlighted by the need for documented, consistent maintenance.

— *Key control*: This is the most obvious countermeasures to crime. Unfortunately, the reverse is also true, and the lack of adequate key control with monumental and often tragic results has many times been the basis for a legal determination that guest protection and reasonable care were not in place. There are those among the lodging industry, otherwise sophisticated hospitality managers, who doubt that key control is possible. They believe that control is impossible, given the numbers and types and movement of property keys. Unfortunately, they sometimes virtually disregard any attempt to manage effectively this countermeasure. With a myriad of keying and locking systems available, from mechanical to electronic, from cards of one construction to several others, the array of problems seems endless.

— *Guest-room protection*: The guest usually spends more time in the guest-room than any other location on the property. The guest is often asleep, obviously, in this guest-room and this is another factor which increases vulnerability. The time spent in the guest-room, for the most part, is during night-time hours—times when traditionally hotel staffing numbers are at their lowest. This reduced staff level also adds to the guest's exposure.

— *Emergency response procedures*: The inclusion of emergency response procedures as a countermeasure may seem a contradiction in terms. Even so, it has been held in court, time and time again, that while the deterrent to incidents against the guest is vital, it is considered equally important that the staff be prepared to respond to emergencies should they arise. An effective emergency response programme, not unlike other countermeasures, begins with the survey.

Role of Protection Management Committee

These committees have addressed the issue of safety that discipline concerned with protecting employees from accidents and injuries. The committees have been composed of representatives from various departments and have traditionally met once or twice a month. Safety has dealt with a concern for protecting an identified asset from an identified threat. It would be unusual to expect to see any agenda item outside the traditional scope of safety. The adoption of the protection management committee model, however, changes the face and effectiveness of this body. A model protection management committee should have the following characters.

— The committee will be composed of representatives from every department on the property.

— The committee will be chaired by the general manager and have the responsibility for establishing and maintaining an acceptable level of protection on the property.

The entire protection management committee must likewise be educated. The general manager can indeed educate them by addressing this entire new concept. He can address it by reminding all of them that they are already managers. As a manager, he should remind them does not act simply as a functionary. Guest protection, then, within that department, is already the housekeeper's responsibility. He can address it by re-emphasizing the value, the advantages and the absolute necessity of guest protection. He addresses it by assuring the group that he has already surveyed each department and each countermeasure, and his survey will act as their road map. The actual process begins when each particular manager accepts his particular countermeasure responsibility.

The full committee has acted as an oversight group. They have addressed the subject countermeasures and collectively decided which are appropriate, necessary, effective, need adjustment or in need of being downgraded. The committee reports to the general manager its findings. The general manager then considers the committee's recommendations, adjudicates, and assigns specific managers to be responsible for specific countermeasures. Certainly a major consideration for selection should be each candidate-manager's strengths and capabilities. Another consideration should be steeped in the realisation that management integration and counterbalance will strengthen the property management profile.

4

Prevention of Hotel Thefts

Security is everyone's job. Successful prevention measures depend on a well-designed programme that involves input from all employees. The security manager can work with employees in a variety of ways.

— He or she should educate employees about the seriousness of theft and how it affects them.

— She or he should attempt to develop employees' understanding of the problem in terms that they as members of the organisation can relate to and appreciate. For example, if it is made clear that all losses cut into the profitability of the property and that reduced profits, if severe enough, may result in lower wages or even laying off employees, the employees may realise that they too have a financial stake in the prevention of losses.

— Assistance from employees may be elicited by encouraging them to call and report suspicious people or circumstances and at least make an extra effort to secure valuables when leaving a work area (for example, securing tools in storage rooms).

— It is essential that the security department maintain a good working relationship with all employees, avoiding morale problems created by poor communications and a lack of understanding. Employees suffering from poor morale are not going to be very concerned about protecting the assets of the employer.

— The security manager must work with all other department managers to get their input on solutions to the problem of losses.

Some security personnel may think that the solution to the loss problem is locking up and limiting access to the hotel's assets, but if a measure interferes with the normal operation of a hotel, it will be resisted and is a guaranteed failure. In fact, the security function will be viewed as less effective unless the solution recommended includes input from the departments affected by it. Programme design is only half of the crime prevention task. The other half, which is equally important, is continuous improvement.

The security manager should repeat the risk survey at least quarterly, if possible, to ensure compliance with the programme, and to discover any changes in the physical structure or the hotel operation that may negate the original plan. The programme must always remain flexible to meet the needs of the business. New and better methods should always be sought for improved preventive measures. When losses do occur, as they will, evaluate the loss and adjust the programme accordingly.

One reason why hotel managers are concerned about the theft of guest property is the potential impact on future business. Legal issues, most states have limited an innkeeper's liability to a fixed amount and generally that amount is not very high. A history of serious guest losses may, however, drastically affect the hotel's reputation and may also be indicative of other weaknesses in the security programme which could lead to more serious crimes.

— Investigation of such losses should include an examination of the locking hardware on the room to ensure that it is working properly. This could be a problem because guests frequently may not close their door tightly when leaving or when running down the hall for ice or soda.

— Determine which employees have access to the room under investigation and note them for further follow-up. If good records are kept, after a short while the same employee's name will begin to appear regularly. Once that is discovered, the investigation could focus more on that individual.

— Find out when the locks were last changed or rekeyed. There may be an overall problem with key control.

— Check for missing room or master keys that anyone could use to gain access to guest rooms.

Prevention of guest room theft depends primarily on employee and guest cooperation. Guest cooperation is more difficult to obtain because of guests' transient nature, but can be achieved to a reasonable extent. The type of cooperation sought is generally limited to two areas: use of existing risk-reducing equipment such as safe deposit boxes and in-room safes, and making sure guests close and properly lock their room doors either when they leave or go to sleep.

Some hotels put small signs or fliers in guest rooms advertising the availability of safe deposit boxes and in-room safes, as well as directions on how to properly secure the door. Other hotels use the cable system on the room television to promote safety and security measures. An employee's personal property, uniforms, and hotel equipment are subject to theft in locker rooms and work areas. Although the theft of such property is not generally seen as a liability problem, it should be of concern from the standpoint of employee morale.

It is a well-known fact that poor employee morale will reduce productivity and will fail to promote the kind of cooperation needed by the security department to prevent other losses. The theft of any employee valuable should be treated with the same level of concern and priority as any other loss. The two most common areas for losses to occur are locker rooms and office areas. In locker rooms, the lockers must be equipped with adequate locks and a sound key control system. Security also should check locker rooms frequently during their patrols. This should be done randomly whenever security personnel are in the immediate area or intentionally as part of the routine patrol.

When time permits, each locker should be checked to ensure it is secured, in addition to seeing that it has regular maintenance and bringing problems of abuse to the security manager's attention. (In some areas it has also been common to put push-button locks on the locker room entrance door to ensure added safety and security to those employees changing in the locker room.) Such inspections also reveal health problems (e.g., pest control) and problems such as stockpiling of uniforms or other hotel equipment (banquet utensils, housekeeping amenities, etc.). Consistent with this approach is the need for a hotel policy on what may be kept in employees' lockers and the hotel's right to search them periodically (a two-person integrity search is recommended).

In office areas, the most frequent loss occurs when employees leave their handbags, wallets, backpacks, briefcases, or gym bags unattended in unlocked desk drawers or on top of desks. The security manager needs to be sure that desks can be locked, and encourage employees to use those locks to protect their personal property. Another common practice is for employees to leave an office door wide open to give a false impression that they are still working, when in fact they have left for the day. Yet in doing this, they may leave their personal effects in plain view for anyone to take easily.

Anytime someone is injured in the hotel or property is lost, security should conduct some form of an investigation. There are at least three advantages of a thorough investigation. First, the root cause of the problem hopefully will be discovered. If, for example, a guest became injured as a result of falling down a stairway, it is important to investigate the root cause of the fall. In such a case, the fall could be caused by torn or worn carpeting, poor lighting, lack of handrails, wet or slippery surfaces, or some factor inherent to the guest.

Some possible reasons for the guest to fall include intoxication, improper footwear, bifocals, or other mobility problems. The same issues are present when an employee is injured on the job. The second reason for a thorough investigation is prevention. By analysing the cause of a theft, for example, security can determine how the article was stolen and then develop preventive measures to avoid similar losses in the future.

The theft of food from kitchen storage areas is common to hotels and restaurants of all sizes. If investigation of this indicates that methods of inventory control are deficient, recommendations can be generated to implement better control and reduce further losses. The security manager who analyses all incidents and implements proactive procedures will prevent incidents of theft. However, employees are constantly developing new methods to steal which, when discovered, should be used as learning tools for security. New methods of theft are usually brought into a facility by a new employee who introduces that method to other employees.

The third benefit gained from an investigation also is related to future loss prevention. In a case of stolen property or drug dealing, for example, the simple process of questioning witnesses and suspects will create a deterrent to future crime. Routinely interviewing potential suspects will help establish an atmosphere of non-tolerance for crime.

Employees who may be guilty of wrongdoing, or who may have considered it, hopefully will be deterred from future activity if the impression is given that the hotel management will not tolerate misconduct. A timely and thorough investigation of every incident, requiring more than just an initial incident report, will enhance the department's image and will help develop an effective security programme.

Chasing suspects, making arrests, and testifying in court are also job responsibilities of a hotel's security staff. For many hotels, though, these activities often are ones of last resort when attempting to address the problem of crime and its associated losses. Although arrests may not be the preferred option of many hotels, they may be necessary and will occur in even the safest properties. Security managers, therefore, need to be prepared to deal with the problems generated by making arrests and prosecuting offenders.

Protecting Guests from Identity Thefts

Personal information was located on the guest folio and was in the hands of a stranger who had ample opportunity to steal the previous guest's identity. This happens all too often in large and small facilities. Identity theft can occur in hotels and motels and should be taken very seriously. Identity fraud is one of the fastest growing white-collar crimes worldwide. Identity thieves capture information about your guests and use it to commit fraud, steal money, and charge items to credit accounts and even create new accounts. How can you protect your patrons and guests from being victims of identity theft? Here are some basic security rules for you to pass on to your managers and supervisors to decrease the likelihood that your patrons and guests will be the next victims of identity theft.

— Training is the most important rule. Hotel personnel should never announce out loud the guest's name and room number at the front desk during check-in or in the food and beverage outlets in the hotel or facility. If during the check-in process, you or any of your employees overhears a guestroom number being announced, immediately assign a different room for the guest. In addition, instruct your wait staff not to request a guest's room number out loud in restaurants. Have the guest write it on a piece of paper then destroy the paper. Never, ever say the room number out loud. Believe it or not, this is still happening at hotels and motels across America.

— Instruct your housekeeping staff to leave a kind note for the guest reminding them to never leave important papers containing personal information in plain view in your guestroom, the lobby, any of the food and beverage outlets or in any meeting room space. Remind them to put all personal information, such as airplane tickets, passports, etc. in the in-room safe located in the guestroom when absent from the room.

— Remind guests, and meeting planners so they can advise their attendees, to make sure all computers, including laptops and PDAs (which usually contain valuable and personal information) are secured in all meeting rooms or hand carried by the owner from the guestroom or meeting room space.

— Have your front office and accounting office procedures that address your efforts to safeguard guests' personal information in writing and available for your guests to see. Find out if there are any leaks or holes in your process. Who has access to guests' data and is it secured? Are the employees trained on maintaining the privacy of guests, and how so and how often? How secure are your fax machines? Does personal guest information lie around for anyone walking by to see? Hotels and motels need to focus on these issues and if you haven't, you need to do so immediately.

— Do not place calls directly to guestrooms without the caller knowing the name of the guest assigned to the guestroom for that day. Although your telephone operators want to be helpful to callers, they should never give out names or partial names of any guests to outside callers.

— Do not slip guestroom folios under the guestroom doors the evening prior to checkout. Mistakes by your night shift hotel staff can and do happen and valuable personal information may find it's way into another guestroom or worse yet, stranded in the middle of the hallway for all guests and employees to see.

— Check the credit card receipts printed from all outlets in your hotel, such as retail shops and restaurants. Some receipts still print the entire credit card numbers. Others only print the last four digits of the credit card number. Having the entire number printed on the receipt can be hazardous to your guests' financial health. This is usually a simple software programming issue and it will protect your guests if you promptly remedy this situation.

— Remind all meeting attendees to remove their convention badges outside the meeting venue as it provides immediate personal information to any stranger the attendee passes by. Also, remind meeting planners to be careful as to what information is stored on the back side of the convention badges because if it is lost or misplaced, the information displayed, albeit intended for the ease and convenience of the attendee (such as cell phone numbers of colleagues), can end up in the wrong hands.

— Inspect your wastepaper refuse system or trash dumpsters for your hotel or facility. It is in a secure area? Is it inaccessible to the general public? Does a fence or wall surround it? If thieves will go through your personal household trash receptacles to gain personal information, imagine what they could find if they gained access to the waste paper dumpster located at your hotel or motel. Some thieves have admitted that they go dumpster diving at accounting and law offices to gain proprietary information. What will they find if they dive into your dumpsters?

— Be aware of the potential for identity theft with your hotel if you engage shoptalk or shop call systems. This is when you contract with a third party provider to record live reservation calls for purposes of spot checking the reservation agents for compliance efforts and for training purposes. These audio recordings which include names, addresses and credit card information are now in the hands of someone, other than the hotel staff, that can abuse the process and use this information to steal personal information. Make sure you have written agreements with these companies, together with clear and precise language in the contracts prohibiting any type of use of the information contained on the tapes. The information on the tapes should be limited to hotel use only.

5

Protecting Hotels and Motels from Terrorism

In everyday business, Hotels need to urgently—and, in many cases, drastically—step up security arrangements and learn to live with the threat of terrorism. With many properties in Asia Pacific carrying the well-known and easily identifiable brands of US and other international brands, they present prime potential targets to terrorists seeking to grab the world's headlines. These were the key messages from the recent HOTEL Asia Pacific Security Workshops, held in Bali and Jakarta. "Hotels, whether or not they are star-rated, must improve safety standards and security systems," Gen Made Mangku Pastika, chief investigator into the Bali bombings, told the delegates. "Otherwise, they must be ready to face disaster, which can happen anywhere and at any time."

Many hotels in Indonesia had not yet been equipped with adequate security and safety systems to counter terror attacks. "At least, they have to meet the minimum standards for required safety and security systems. They have to spend extra money on it. "Employees must be trained to become the first line of defence. In order to prevent further tragedies, we need the full cooperation of the industry."

Pastika's warnings, although specifically aimed at hotels in Indonesia, were echoed by other speakers, whose comments had wider geographical relevance. Chester Doty, group director of security for Shangri-La Hotels and Resorts, said: "We have to reassure both our guests and our staff that they are getting the best security we can provide them. He pinpointed a number of issues that need to be addressed by the industry, including:

— Growing political, ethnic and religious tensions [in Indonesia, Malaysia and the Philippines];

— Ensuring that employees and physical assets are protected for many reasons – including insurance liability and premiums;

— Evaluating and putting technology in place to address the new security challenges.

— There is no such thing as enough training and, no matter how much technology a hotel installs, it is only as effective as the people," said Doty.

— Before 9/11, security was the unwanted stepchild of the hotel industry, because it did not make money. Now, all that has changed and security is right in the spotlight.

Security has now entered the thinking man's arena—and we have to think out of the box. Craig Foster, regional director of leading security consultancy Hill & Associates, discussed the crucial importance of crisis management, which he defined as "an event, or set of circumstances, that threatens the integrity, reputation or survival of an individual or organisation" or as a "decisive moment, time of great danger or great difficulty".

"A crisis can put at risk a hotel's two most important tangibles: its corporate reputation and its brand image. "There is little that can be done to affect the threat, so actions must concentrate on reducing the vulnerability."

All hotels should develop policies, procedures, plans, teams and facilities to "mitigate the risks or minimise the consequences".

"It is crucial to identify preparatory steps before a crisis, strike a balance between too much and too little detail, coordinate input from different agencies and departments, and make critical decisions in advance."

Timothy Dumas, regional security officer attached to the US Embassy in Jakarta, said: "Terrorism is no longer simply a government concern. Gone are days when only government establishments were targets – today, everything from hotels to nightclubs to schools is a potential target. "Cooperation among intelligence agencies around the world has expanded to unprecedented levels. Planned attacks have been prevented and lives have been saved, but incidents such as the Bali and Kenya bombings show us more work still needs to be done.

"Hotels offer excellent potential targets for a variety of reasons. They must remain open, there are many people moving around and there are many entrances and exits. It is very difficult to prevent an attack if someone is determined." James Filgo, Asia Pacific director of Consolidated Services International, gave a number of pointers on training staff as the first line of defence.

"Security is the main concern of guests these days, and quality hotels are expected to have in place high standards, policies and procedures. "Impressions count, and hotel staff either give a sense of security or insecurity." Filgo said that hotels were liable for staff inaction or errors, and that security was "too all-persuasive to limit to security personnel alone". "Security training is essential for all staff, and requires a top-down approach in which every function is subordinate to guest protection."

Filgo urged all hotels to establish a Protection Management Committee (PMC) responsible for:

— Conducting a security/diagnostic survey, involving both the GM and the security manager;
— Completing a threat assessment report;
— Reviewing each threat compared to each asset;
— Collectively determining completeness of the security survey and threat assessment;
— Allocate responsibilities for each counter-measure selected.

Action plan counter-measures should include:
— Pre-employment screening;
— Staff-wide training;
— Access control;
— Key control;
— Security officers;
— Guestroom protection and
— Emergency response.

Better Safety and Security in Hotel near Airports

Hotels near airports offer the most safety and security features, with large hotels, luxury hotels of any size and new hotels also ranking high on the safety and security indexes devised by Cathy Enz, a professor at Cornell University's School of Hotel Administration, and Masako Taylor, a Ph.D. candidate at the school. Enz, who is director of the Hotel School's Center for Hospitality Research, said: "A significant proportion of the 2,123 hotels included in our study rated 85 percent or higher on our indexes, which looked at such features as security camera monitoring systems, secured corridors, electronic locks and sprinkler systems. That news is reassuring now that we're seeing a heightened concern among the general public about how safe we are in public buildings, including hotels."

In general, the newer the hotel, the higher its safety and security scores, the researchers found. "This is probably because electronic locks, sprinklers and interior corridors are relatively less common in older hotels than in hotels built in the last decade," said Enz. Luxury hotels are the exception, she noted. "Because they are renovated frequently, even the oldest ones are likely to have the latest safety and security features." Accordingly, after airport hotels, luxury and upscale hotels had the highest scores for safety and security. All-suite properties and convention hotels also scored high.

While resorts scored low on the physical safety and security features, Enz attributed some of that result to customer demands for such amenities as rooms that open onto balconies overlooking such public areas as pools or the ocean. "It may be that what we want in a resort, we don't want in urban hotel properties," Enz said.

Motels had the lowest safety and security score, and bed-and-breakfast properties and condominiums also scored low, most likely because many lack sprinklers and electronic door locks, Enz commented. In an earlier survey published in February 2002, Enz found hotel general managers reported few changes in safety and security measures or added security staff members following the terrorist attacks of Sept. 11. "While no place is immune to danger, taken together the two studies suggest that hotels had already implemented many of the safety and security features we found in our new survey and were fairly safe, secure places to begin with," said Enz.

Enz and Taylor used data from the 2001 American Hotel & Lodging Survey prepared by RealTime Hotel Reports, which is part of Smith Travel Research. The researchers checked for these five key safety features:

sprinklers, smoke detectors, in-room safety information, safety videos and security cameras; and these five security features: electronic locks, interior corridors, security cameras, in-room safety information and a safety video. They gave a weighted score for each feature to create separate safety and security indexes, each with a potential perfect score of 100.

Legal Status of Hotel Owners

Atrocities in the US and Indonesia have focused the hotel industry's mind on the "terror risks" of doing business, with both owners and managers facing unprecedented challenges. But what is their legal status should the unthinkable happen at one of their properties? Over the past two years, one defined term and certain "esoteric provisions" in these agreements have achieved "special-significance status".

These clauses address the circumstances under which the parties to the contract may be excused from non-performance, or may even have the right to terminate the agreement, without liability. Other provisions, which no doubt have been scrutinised more carefully, are the "damage, destruction and condemnation" clauses which set out the situations where a hotel owner is obliged to repair its hotel if it is damaged. These provisions have become crucial in allocating the respective liabilities of an owner and an operator if the hotel they own and operate is affected, damaged or even destroyed as a result of a terrorist attack.

An owner might think that having his hotel destroyed by a terrorist attack would be unfortunate enough. To rub salt into the owner's financial wound, though, he may actually be contractually bound to repair the property, even if he would otherwise have preferred to turn it to some other use after the tragedy. The obligation of an owner to repair the hotel under a management agreement usually depends on the extent of the damage. In general, if the costs of repair do not exceed a certain threshold specified in the management agreement [which is usually a certain percentage of the replacement costs of the hotel], the owner will be obliged to repair the hotel to its condition prior to the destruction.

However, if the costs of repair exceed the specified threshold, the owner will have the right to choose not to undertake the repair and to terminate the management agreement. Another threshold may also be negotiated in respect of the obligation to repair when the damage is not covered by insurance. The determination of these thresholds is a matter for the owner and operator to negotiate.

In a dramatic case in which a hotel is "appropriated" by an army, hostage situation or other "forceful authority", an owner will generally have the right to terminate the management agreement if the hotel is taken for a long period of time, as specified in the agreement. If the length of "appropriation" is shorter than the specified period, the obligation of the owner to repair and reinstate the hotel after the "appropriation" will usually depend on the cost of repair, as discussed above.

Loss of Money

The damage caused by terrorism to the hotel industry are far more extensive than mere physical property damage. The impact of the recent bombing outside the JW Marriott Jakarta has had an impact on the hospitality industry in Indonesia, which is still struggling to recover from the aftermath of the Bali bombing and the more recent problems caused by SARS. During the downturn of local, regional and global tourism—with the resulting decreased turnover and revenues an owner, typically, will be most concerned as to how operating expenses can continue to be funded.

Generally, in most hotel-management agreements, there is no limitation on the owner's obligation to fund working capital. In other words, there is an open-ended requirement on the owner to contribute. Very often, an owner is unable to rely on the force-majeure clause to avoid or delay making such contributions. Most force-majeure provisions would not excuse a failure to make any monetary payments, even when unforeseeable and uncontrollable events occur. It is worth pointing out that force-majeure clauses, like all other provisions, are meant to reflect the intentions of the parties, and can be drafted and/or varied as they wish - no doubt following prolonged negotiation of these terms.

From an operator's perspective, when a hotel's business is affected by terrorism, a direct and immediate consequence is the reduction of management fees, which are usually calculated on the basis of gross revenues or gross operating profits. Quite apart from that, the operator might also have to face the pressure of meeting the performance tests or guarantees set out in the management agreements. In many agreements, there is a requirement for operators to meet minimum performance standards or performance guarantees, and a failure to do so may entitle the owners to terminate the management agreements.

Obviously terrorism has caused a number of hotels around the world to fall short of these agreed performance targets. Performance-test-related provisions which are carefully drafted, however, would usually provide some "reasonable" exceptions under which the operator will not be held responsible for a failure to meet the performance test. These exceptions generally include:

— Loss of business due to major renovations of the hotel;
— Failure to meet targets due to force majeure events; and
— Where failure is attributable to any event of default by the owner.

Any reasonable force-majeure provision would also cover acts of terrorism. In some management agreements, in addition to the exceptions briefly described above, operators may also have the choice of avoiding termination by making a "Cure Payment"—or some other payment—to meet any shortfall due under the performance guarantee.

If a hotel is destroyed by acts of terrorism, another issue which owners and operators might have to tackle is potential claims brought by guests for injuries caused. Generally, neither the operator nor the owner would be held liable for any injury or death caused by terrorist activities, unless the owner or operator has failed to exercise reasonable care for the safety and security of their guests. Therefore, to make sure that the reasonable-care standard is met, it is necessary and advisable for owners and operators to take reasonable and necessary steps to protect the safety of guests, including implementing appropriate security policies and measures and providing crisis-management training to all employees.

The events of 9/11 have brought significant changes to the insurance industry. While it is generally still possible to obtain terrorism insurance coverage in the market, the high cost of such coverage in some countries has driven many hotels to reluctantly raise their risk tolerance level and forego such insurance coverage. Of course, this means that when a hotel incurs any liability arising from terrorist attacks, these liabilities—which could be enormous—will be borne entirely by the owner unless the government of the country in which the hotel is located steps in to meet this liability or to provide other financial support.

While contract and insurance might address some issues relating to terrorism, they are not perfect solutions. To protect their own interests, operators and owners must apply more resources and attention to safety and security issues to minimise the risks of terrorist attacks in their hotels, or at least mitigate the damage in the unfortunate occurrence of such attacks.

6

Electronic Safety in Hotels

Evolution of Electronic Lock

The evolution of the electronic door locking industry began with guest security, and expanded to increase operational efficiencies available to property management through access control and system integration. The industry now stands poised to enter the new millennium as a major technology provider, positioning hotels as key players in an era of increased electronic commerce. Few inventions have had such widespread and practical appeal to the hospitality industry. Since the introduction of the recodable electronic door lock in the late 1970's, hotel security has been virtually transformed. The focus at the time of inception was increased guest security, but the benefit to the property was quickly realised.

Hotel security experts, along with media pundits, the courts, and the insurance industry all agree - keycard locks, which can be easily changed so that every guest gets a new key, are the best way to boost security. In fact, there is speculation that by the end of this decade, hotels that do not feature electronic locking mechanisms in guestrooms will be unable to obtain insurance. Even the simplest of key card locks have been found to reduce break ins by up to 80%, reminding us that effective guestroom security is an essential part of the hospitality package.

Employee access control was one of the first system enhancements to increase the level of internal technology. In order for a property to be maintained efficiently, hotel personnel require their own means of entry to rooms in which they must perform daily routines or tasks. In the past, distribution of conventional keys to housekeepers, room service attendants, and maintenance personnel compromised guest belongings and increased the liability of the hotel. In some instances of theft, the victim was often the hotel (where even the negligent customer is king), and claims went unchallenged.

The "burden of proof" is welcome by a hotel equipped with modern electronic locks, for the actual lock serves as a log, monitoring and recording up to 1,000 entries (about 100 days worth). Many reputations have been restored and many a thankful employee has been cleared of suspicion due to the success of these products. Employee key cards can be coded to allow access only to their assigned units of responsibility and only during the hours of their shift. Knowledge of these system capabilities may also serve as a deterrent to those less ethical.

At ILCO UNICAN, true on-line security systems are giving hotel operators even greater peace of mind. Tom Caudill, VP of Sales and Marketing Worldwide for Lodging Products, describes the additional safety features of a monitoring system providing the status of every lock in the hotel. Information conveyed by this system can be used to determine the occupancy of a room, which can be communicated with energy management systems. Doors left ajar transmit an alarm, and a courtesy call ensues. Master keys can be disengaged instantly from the main console, without having to delete the sequence from each lock, (a tedious task deplored by the Director of Security).

"Smart card" is a generic term for a card the size and thickness of a credit or debit card embedded with a microprocessor chip. The chip itself has intelligence and computational power similar to that of early personal computers. These powerful processing capabilities make smart cards much more secure than other types of cards presently in use. They can handle encryption techniques that protect the information stored on the cards. Think of a smart card as a very small personal computer belonging only to you. Because it's small enough to fit in your wallet, it's portable. And like a personal computer, it can be programmed to serve many different purposes and do many different things.

Smart cards are currently being used to secure financial transactions, as stored value cards, for insurance identification, to store medical information and to personalise cellular phone communication from anywhere in the world. The beauty of the smart card is that it can offer all of these applications with considerable information storage capacity and security. Phil Wilder, Director of Marketing for San Diego-based Computerised Security Systems, believes that the value added by smart card technology offers the hotel operator "a revolutionary new way of marketing and merchandising to the guest".

In a world moving towards one-to-one marketing, smart cards hold the capability to customise and better serve individual needs. The smart card can carry information that is only yours, such as travel preferences and loyalty program account information. Programs and incentives are easily tailored to guests based on their own usage patterns of hotel services. Smart cards can also provide more privacy and security in accessing payments and information services, because the microprocessor chip that holds the information cannot be easily duplicated.

In July of 1998, Hilton Hotels International announced that the Hilton New York & Towers, the largest hotel in

New York City, would become the first hotel in the nation to install a locking system fully integrated with true smart card capacity. There are an estimated 6,000 travellers who already carry credit cards with smart card technology. Holders of the American Express™ Corporate Card, Hilton Optima™ Card and Hilton HHonors™ Worldwide Diamond VIP member cards will be able to present these cards upon check in to be coded as their room access keys. With time, it is anticipated that these same cards will be used at check-in kiosks located in hotel lobbies or airport terminals, expediting the check- in process.

Network and personal computer usage is one of the major applications driving smart cards, along with PCs, Internet access, security and financial applications. As more people utilise electronic commerce (shopping over the Internet), more secure methods of electronic payment will be demanded from these consumers. Self-proclaimed "futurist" Steve Hovanitz, Vice President of Sales & Marketing for Vingcard, envisions the following scenario made possible by smart card technology. A business traveller uses his personal computer, with smart card reader, to buy an airline ticket and reserve a hotel room. Information transmitted through the Internet includes his frequent flyer number, as well as his credit card information to secure payment.

Accommodation preference and loyalty program account information is also communicated electronically to the hotel booking service. Confirmation information is written to the smart card, and upon arrival at the airport, the card is used to obtain a boarding pass from an automated system. At his destination, the traveller proceeds to the hotel check-in kiosk, located perhaps within the airport. Smart card is inserted to retrieve room assignment, secure payment, maybe even reward the loyal guest with a beverage value credited to his card. The same card is encoded with the room access information, and the card further serves as the key, allowing the guest to bypass the front desk entirely.

Smart card applications heighten internal operational technology as well. Let's revisit employee access systems with Paul Zimmerman, Technical Director for North America at TimeLox. The world's largest hotel development to date, The Venetian (where else but Las Vegas), has just selected TimeLox to fit 6,000+ guestrooms and employee areas with the company's DC-One System. The employee key card, traditionally identifies and controls access for authorised personnel; with smart card technology, the card becomes a walking production database. Reports generated from a maintenance engineer's smart card help verify work order fulfillment, by indicating whether or not a service call was placed to a specific room.

Before the travel and tourism industry can see the full benefit of smart card technology, standards must be defined and upheld by the banking and software industries. It is important to observe that smart card technology may never take hold of our population, as it has in many European countries. Tom Caudill, (ILCO UNICAN) reminds us that the proliferation of smart card technology elsewhere is a result of less sophisticated information infrastructures. Information must be carried individually, because centralised data access and storage is not as reliable or efficient in other countries.

The hospitality industry has historically been on the lagging edge of technology. From a service perspective, there has been a reluctance to embrace technology that makes any guest transaction less personal. Economically, the cost of keeping up with technology has often outweighed the benefits for an industry that relies so much on its human elements.

The electronic locking industry is helping us transition, by incorporating new and exciting technology into an amenity that hotels cannot be without. Electronic door lock makers are preparing for society's acceptance and increased reliance upon a technological prophesy that has yet to be fulfilled. However, proponents insist that the value added for consumers of these systems, is product readiness in a quickly changing world obsessed with convenience and security.

7

Food Safety Issues

Food safety, will refer to the handling of food and food contact items in a manner that reduces the risk of a foodborne illness outbreak. Food safety buzz is everywhere. It is a regular story for local news programs throughout the country. Equal attention is being given to the topic by foodservice equipment and supplies manufacturers, as they are eager to develop tools to assist with the implementation of safe food handling practices. Likewise, local health department inspectors and industry associations who promote food safety education are making sure that the topic's importance is clearly conveyed.

New food safety related requirements are rarely communicated clearly and expectations are rarely addressed with end users. Another reason that the implementation of safe food handling practices has been difficult is ... money. It seems as though several members of the hospitality industry have focused on the potential profit from food safety related efforts first, and the benefits of food safety implementation second.

Implementing food safety principles makes good business sense. Sure, there may be some costs involved ... but look at the alternatives. What is the cost of a foodborne illness outbreak? Or, how about losing the stigma that food safety is a hush-hush topic and advertising your efforts to your customers. Let them know you are working your tail off to provide safe food. They will appreciate it.

Most food becomes "unsafe" through cross-contamination, the contact of food or food contact surfaces that are sanitary with those that possess organisms. The best way to prevent cross-contamination is proper receiving ... never let the contaminated product enter your facility. This is your first and best line of defense. To assist with this effort, a proper receiving area should be designed and included in every foodservice facility, regardless of size.

Should contaminated product slip through the back door, certain key design elements can help reduce the risk of cross contamination. First, be sure that your facility's design follows the flow of the food through the facility. In other words, limit or eliminate the possibility that potentially hazardous and ready-to-eat products will cross paths. By preventing the crossing of flow patterns in the kitchen, the risk of cross contamination is reduced.

Next, provide separate food preparation areas for potentially hazardous and non-hazardous foods, and separate these areas with physical barriers. For instance, provide separate vegetable and meat/fish/poultry preparation areas with a physical element between them. It is awful tough for chicken juice splatter to go through a wall and come in contact with ready-to-eat vegetables. Wallah ... cross contamination is prevented. The same principles of separation apply to the ware washing section of the kitchen, an area prone to cross contamination. Given the quantity of soiled and clean product in one confined area, separation is critical in ware washing.

Specific equipment may also be provided within a foodservice facility to assist with safe food handling practices. Such equipment selections include hands-free hand sinks and blast chillers, amongst many others. Hand sinks operated by electronic eye, foot lever, or knee valve activation reduce cross contamination that can occur from touching the faucet handles. The blast chiller is designed to reduce the internal temperature of a product to a safe temperature (below 41°F) in a time period that complies with food safety standards. Even if the unit is not purchased right away, providing the utility requirements during renovation or construction can save a great deal of money and provide valuable benefits down the road.

Proper storage, whether of food or pots, pans, and utensils, is important as well. With regards to food, raw product should always be stored below cooked product. Separate shelving colors or shelf labels can be used to ensure that this practice is followed. In conjunction with operational procedures, these design components can assist in providing a safer product for the customer. Take a look at your facility. Are you preventing cross contamination … by design?

Violation of Food Safety: A Case Study of Restaurants in South Mississippi

The violations documented by health inspectors are enough to turn diners' stomachs — rats nibbling on hamburger buns, raw chicken juices dripping onto precooked foods and kitchen employees changing their shoes and handling food without washing their hands. And the problems are happening over and over. Since 2001, state Health Department records show that South Mississippi restaurants have committed nearly 3,500 "critical" violations, those most likely to make diners sick.

In fact, a Sun Herald computer analysis of health inspection reports shows that, between Jan. 1, 2001 and May 31, 2002, one of every three restaurants in Hancock, Harrison, Jackson, George, Pearl River and Stone counties failed at least one inspection. The Health Department closed nine restaurants during that time period.

Serious mistakes were not limited to chronic offenders. Inspectors found critical violations at virtually every type of restaurant, from fast-food joints to fine-dining spots. Consumers, though, are often oblivious to whether a restaurant has been deemed unsafe, although the Health Department recently began putting the scores on an Internet site.

While health inspectors would like to do more to make restaurants safer, they say they simply don't have the manpower to step up their enforcement efforts. The number of food establishments in the area has doubled in the last 10 years. But state legislators have not provided the local Health Department with additional funds to hire new inspectors.

And without the proper vigilance, inspectors warn that virtually any mistake by a restaurant, even a minor one, could lead to diners getting food poisoning. "It takes just one incident to cause an outbreak," said Melissa Mixon, a food safety professor with the Mississippi State University Extension Services. "So these restaurants cannot afford to be sloppy." So, should you think twice before dining out? Probably not. Since 2001, the reports indicate that 85 percent of food establishments in South Mississippi passed their inspections.

Diners usually can't tell from a casual glance whether a restaurant has problems. Inspectors, on the other hand, come armed with a 43-point checklist from the Food and Drug Administration and scrutinize every aspect of a restaurant's operations. They check food temperatures with a thermometer, poke through cabinets for roach droppings and observe whether employees wear gloves or wash their hands when they're supposed to.

The inspection process, having evolved in recent years, now focuses mostly on catching and correcting the 13 different critical violations, such as foods kept at temperatures that can promote bacteria growth or juices from raw meats dripping onto ready-to-eat foods. Restaurants that get even one critical violation can fail their inspection. Health Department officials, however, have some discretion in determining what constitutes a violation. For instance, if a mistake occurs that can be corrected, such as an out-of-temperature food that can discarded before reaching diners, the inspector usually will not count it against them.

When a restaurant fails an inspection, health officials return within 10 days for a follow-up inspection. Thus, restaurants with more problems typically get more frequent inspections. Critical violations, though, do occur frequently. During The Sun Herald's review of 6,000 inspections completed at 1,440 South Mississippi restaurants, at least one critical violation was found in about one out of three inspection reports. The most common critical violations:

— Food temperature problems were found in 668 inspections. This violation occurs when food temperatures get into the danger area between 41 degrees and 140 degrees, a range that is ripe for bacteria growth. The Health Department's mantra: cold food must be kept cold and hot food must be kept hot.

— Hygiene problems were found in 650 inspections. This violation occurs when employees don't wash their hands or fail to put on gloves when handling foods, which could spread harmful bacteria or viruses.

— Cross-contamination violations were found in 487 reports. This violation occurs when potentially dangerous foods, such as raw meats, chicken or seafood, are not stored properly, posing a risk of spreading harmful bacteria to other pre-cooked or ready-to-eat foods.

In the past, inspectors often had difficulty getting some restaurants to break free from patterns in which the same problem continually reappeared. A new regulation, however, now requires those restaurants to submit a "risk control plan," which outlines changes the restaurant will make to avoid the problem in the future. If the problem continues even after a risk control plan is submitted, inspectors are not shy about using their more formidable enforcement tool: Forcing a restaurant to close.

Restaurant closures were once few and far between. It wasn't that restaurants were better maintained, but rather regulations were more relaxed. And local and state politicians, wanting to maintain friendly ties to their constituents, often put the heat on inspectors who closed a restaurant in their area.

"When you close a restaurant down, people take great exception to that," said Dr. Robert Travnicek, South Mississippi's health officer. "So I wouldn't call us the most popular people." But as the rest of the nation became more aware of the risks posed by food-borne illness — especially in 1993 when more than 700 people were sickened in an E.Coli outbreak linked to beef served at Jack in the Box restaurants — Mississippi officials began to take notice.

In the past five years, state health officials have instituted a series of changes in the way restaurants are inspected and have tightened food-safety regulations. The biggest of these, in terms of enforcement, was a regulation from May 2001 that said any restaurant that collects six or more critical violations during an inspection should be shut down on the spot.

China Garden restaurant in Ocean Springs, for example, has been closed three times since 2001 due to the six criticals rule. (One of the closures happened after The Sun Herald's study period.) The most frequently cited mistakes consist of foods left out of temperature, roaches found in dry storage rooms and employees handling ready-to-eat products without gloves.

Maddox said the restaurant's prep coolers were old and couldn't generate enough cool air to keep food cold when the kitchen was ablaze with the preparation of stir-fry dishes. In addition, many of the employees do not understand English, rendering it difficult for inspectors to get their food safety message across. Inspectors said Xin Chen, China Garden's owner, has worked with them to improve conditions at the restaurant. But with each new inspection, the problems seemed to return.

Recently, however, inspectors brought in a translator and put the restaurant's kitchen staff through a food-safety training session in their native language, Mandarin. In addition, Chen said he's made new changes, including the installation of a new prep-cooler and having the place sprayed by exterminators, that will improve the restaurant's safety record. Inspectors think restaurant sanitation would improve if only the Health Department had more manpower. "The only reason we're not getting better is that we're so critically short-staffed," Maddox said. "We can't hire more staff unless we get the money to do it."

8

Preventing Accidents in Hotels and Restaurants

The hotel and restaurant industries employ a large number of young workers. This probably reflects the seasonal and part-time nature of staffing needs in these industries. They require more employees during the summer and weekends—times when young people are typically available to work. Workers of all ages are at risk of being seriously injured on the job in the hotel and restaurant industries, but the large number of young people employed in them highlights the importance of understanding the special concerns with working youth.

Types of Accidents

Thee are the four most common types of accidents:

— Overexertion—These are injuries resulting from the application of force to an object or person—such as lifting, pushing, pulling, and carrying.

— Being struck by an object—With this type of accident, the worker is injured by a moving object such as equipment and tools.

— Falls on the same level— for example, slips.

— Falls from elevations

Overexertion

The following is a breakdown of overexertion accidents by the type of object handled:

— Handling containers. Boxes, cartons, garbage cans or bags, trays, luggage or baggage, and buckets are examples of common containers.

— Moving fixtures and furniture (for example, beds, mattresses, tables, and sofas).

— Handling laundry.

— Handling carts or grocery buggies.

Struck-by Accidents

Being struck by an object or equipment caused of all time-loss claims in the hotel industry. The types of equipment most often involved in these accidents were:

— Knives

— Food containers (for example, dishes, bowls, bottles, jars)

— Furniture (for example, tables, chairs, beds)

Falls on the Same Level

More than half were due to slippery surfaces, and from tripping or rough surfaces. Women had claims for falls on the same level two and a half times more often than men.

Falls from Elevation

Ten percent of all time-loss claims in the hotel industry were falls from elevation.

Violence and Force

Workplace violence has become a growing concern for the

hotel industry. The occupations with the most workplace violence accidents were:

— Bouncers, door attendants
— Bartenders
— Wait staff
— Desk clerks, reservation clerks

Accidents in Restaurant Industry

There are the four most common types of accidents in the restaurant industry:

1. Being struck by an object—These are accidents where the worker is injured by a moving object such as equipment and tools.
2. Falls on the same level
3. Burns and scalds
4. Overexertion—These are injuries resulting from the application of force to an object or person—such as lifting, pushing, pulling, and carrying.

Struck-by Accidents

Accidents with a knife accounted for more than 60 percent of these struck-by accidents. The occupations with the most struck-by accidents were:

— Chefs and cooks
— Kitchen helpers or bus persons

Falls on the Same Level

The occupations with the most falls on the same level were:

— Kitchen helpers or bus persons

— Wait staff
— Chefs and cooks

Burns and Scalds

The occupations with the most burns were:

— Chefs and cooks
— Kitchen helpers or bus persons
— Wait staff

Please note that chemical burns, such as those that janitorial workers could experience when handling chemical cleaning products, are not included in this category. Chemical burns are included in statistics on toxic exposures.

Overexertion

The occupations with the most overexertion accidents were:

— Chefs and cooks
— Kitchen helpers or bus persons
— Wait staff

Prevention of Accidents

In the fast-paced environment of hotels and restaurants, a common attitude is that accidents are inevitable and a part of doing business. But injuries mean losses. Lost money, lost time, and lost productivity. And more importantly, they mean that workers and their families suffer pain and have their lives disrupted. If accidents are prevented, the savings can be significant—less overtime, less retraining, and less time spent investigating accidents, to name a few. The other benefits are also rewarding—morale improves and workers feel valued.

Hotels and restaurants take pride in the service they offer tourists and other customers. Sometimes employees take customer satisfaction so seriously, they think of their customers' safety before their own. Hotels and restaurants could prevent many workplace injuries by paying the same kind of attention to employee health and safety as they do to customer satisfaction.

Tips for Preventing Common Accidents

The safety tips for preventing accidents that commonly occur in the hotel and restaurant industries. Safety tips are included on:

— Cuts

— Knives

— Slips and falls

— Floors

— Stairways

— Storage areas

— Burns and scalds

— Ladders

Cuts

Cuts can occur from:

— Knives

— Furniture

— Equipment

— Counters

— Utensils

— Glassware

— Preparation areas

— Dishes
— Cleaning equipment

Do

— Throw away broken or chipped glassware.
— Use a cutting board for safe cutting and chopping.
— Lock out or disconnect the power source before cleaning equipment such as meat slicers.
— Make sure that you receive proper training in operating equipment and safe job procedures.
— Consult the manufacturer's instruction manual for operating, cleaning, and maintaining the equipment. Make sure that cutting blades are sharp.
— After cleaning, make sure that all guards and safety devices are put back in place.
— Place a warning tag on defective and unsafe equipment and do not re-start the equipment. Inform your supervisor.

Do not

— Do not operate equipment if you feel unwell or drowsy.
— Do not place hands near the edge of cutting blades. Make sure you can always see both hands (and all fingers) and the cutting blades.
— Do not try to catch falling objects.
— Do not try to clean or "just brush something off" a moving part such as cutting blades or beaters in mixers.
— Do not push or place your hand in feed hoppers or delivery chutes. Use food pushers.

— Do not try to cut anything in a slicer that becomes too thin. Use a knife to finish cutting.
— Do not wear loose or frayed clothing, gloves, or jewellery that can be caught in a moving machine.

Knives

Potential injuries: cuts and amputation.

Do

— Use the right knife for the job.
— Always use a proper chopping board or block.
— Make sure the knife is sharp.
— Carry only one knife at a time, tip pointed down at your side.
— Store knives securely in proper racks in a visible place.
— Hold the knife with your stronger hand.
— Cut away from your body when cutting, trimming, or boning.
— When not using knives, place them at the back, with the sharp edge away from you.
— After using a knife, clean it immediately or place it in a dishwasher.
— Use protective clothing such as mesh gloves.

Do not

— Do not leave a knife in dishwater.
— Do not use a knife as a can opener.
— Do not try to catch a falling knife. Let it fall and then pick it up.
— Do not engage in horseplay with a knife in your hand.

— Do not carry knives while carrying other objects.
— Do not carry a knife in your pocket.
— Do not leave knives where they could be accidentally covered.
— Do not talk to your co-workers while you are using a knife—you could become distracted.

Slips and Falls

Slips and falls can occur from:

— Slippery and cluttered floors and stairs
— Loose or bumpy carpets and floor mats
— Defective ladders and footstools
— Poor visibility

Do

— Keep floors and stairs clean, dry, and non-slippery.
— Keep floors and stairs clear of debris and obstruction.
— Use slip-resistant waxes to polish and treat floors.
— Make sure that carpeting, rugs, and mats are free of holes, loose threads, loose edges, and bumps that may cause tripping.
— Use adequate warning signs for wet floors and other hazards.
— Make sure that wooden duckboards and railings are in good repair and free of splinters.
— Make sure that ladders and footstools are in good repair and have non-skid feet.
— If possible, immediately remove or clean up any tripping or slipping hazard you notice. If it's not possible to take care of the hazard yourself, report it immediately to your supervisor.

Do not

— Do not use defective ladders or footstools.
— Do not use chairs, stools, or boxes as substitutes for ladders.
— Do not leave oven, dishwasher, or cupboard doors open. These may present a tripping hazard for you or your co-workers.

Floors

Potential accidents: slips and falls.

Do

— Make sure that walking surfaces are uncluttered, non-slippery, clean, and adequately lighted.
— If you drop or spill something, clean it up immediately.
— Mop floors with the recommended amount of cleaning product in the water, or cleaning fluid, to ensure grease and other slippery substances are removed.
— Make sure floors are free from trip hazards such as raised or broken sections.
— Treat floors with slip-resistant products if the floors must be waxed.
— Place wet floor warning signs to prevent people from slipping.
— Use non-slip mats and floor finishes.
— Replace doormats regularly.
— Walk—don't run.
— Mark swinging doors with in and out signs.

Do not

— Do not leave carts, boxes, trash cans, or other objects on the floors and in the aisles.

Stairways

Potential accidents: slips and falls.

Do

— Ensure that stairways are well lit.

— Keep stairs clear of obstructions.

— Use handrails.

— When carrying a load up and down stairs, make sure that the load does not block your vision. Report tripping hazards to your supervisor and place warning signs.

Do not

— Do not store boxes and supplies on the stairs.

— Do not throw things up or down stairways.

— Do not switch off lights in the stairways.

Storage Areas

Potential hazards: collapse of stored goods; slipping and tripping.

Do

— Make sure the shelves are firmly secured in place against walls and on the floor.

— Ensure adequate lighting.

- — Store chemicals, detergents, and pesticides in a separate area away from foodstuff.
- — Ensure that chemicals that are not compatible with each other are not stored together.
- — Store heavy items on lower shelves, particularly when cartons contain fluids.
- — Use bins and racks as much as possible.
- — Leave adequate clearance space between the top of the stored goods and the ceiling in areas protected by a sprinkler system.
- — Store cartons in dry areas.

Do not

- — Do not block passages in the storage area.
- — Do not stack loose items on the top shelves.
- — Do not overload shelving units.
- — Do not store cardboard cartons in damp areas.
- — Do not overstock.

Ladders

Potential accidents: falls from portable ladders; splinters; slipping.

Do

- — Inspect a ladder before and after each use.
- — Reject a ladder if it has loose, broken, or missing rungs; loose hinges; or loose or missing screws or bolts.
- — Reject and tag defective ladders. Have defective ladders repaired or thrown out.

- Use a ladder designed for your task.
- Consider strength, type, and Canadian Standards Association (CSA) or American National Standards Institute (ANSI) approval.
- Set up barricades and warning signs when using a ladder in a doorway or passageway.
- Clean muddy or slippery footwear before mounting a ladder.
- Face the ladder when going up or down and when working from it.
- Keep the centre of your body within the side rails.
- Place ladder feet 30 cm (1 ft.) from the wall for every 1 m (3 ft.) of height.
- Extend the ladder at least 1 m (3 ft.) above the landing platform.
- Locate the ladder on a firm footing using slip-resistant feet or secure blocking, or have someone hold the ladder.
- Rest both side rails on a top support, and secure the ladder to prevent slipping.
- Use a three-point stance, keeping both feet and at least one hand on the ladder at all times.

Do not

- Do not use ladder in a horizontal position as a scaffold plank or runway.
- Do not carry objects in your hands while on a ladder. Hoist materials or attach tools to a belt.
- Do not work from the top two rungs. The higher you go on a ladder, the greater the possibility that the ladder will slip out at the base.

— Do not use makeshift items such as a chair, barrel, milk crate, or box as a substitute for a ladder.

Burns and Scalds

Burns and scalds can occur from: stoves, toasters, toaster ovens, ovens, boiling hot liquid, hot utensils, pressure cookers, cooking pots, hot dishwashers etc.

Do

— Assume that all pots and pans and metal handles are hot. Touch them only when you are sure that they are not hot or when you are using proper gloves.

— Organize your work area to prevent contact with hot objects and flames.

— Keep pot handles away from hot burners.

— Make sure that handles of pots and pans do not stick out from the counter or cooking stove. Use oven mitts appropriate for handling hot objects. Use long gloves for deep ovens.

— Follow electric and fire safety guidelines.

— Follow the manufacturer's operating instructions.

— Use only recommended temperature settings for each type of cooking.

— Open hot water and hot liquid faucets slowly to avoid splashes.

— Lift lids by opening away from you.

— Wear long-sleeved cotton shirts and cotton pants.

— Report problems to your supervisor.

Do not

— Do not overfill pots and pans.

— Do not leave metal spoons in pots and pans while cooking.
— Do not spill water in hot oil.
— Do not overstretch over a stove, grill, or other hot area in order to reach an uncomfortable distance.
— Do not use a wet cloth to lift lids from hot pots.
— Do not open cookers and steam ovens that are under pressure.
— Do not lean over pots of boiling liquids.
— Do not leave a hot electric element or gas flame of stove "on" all the time.

Role of Young Workers

Workers of all ages face hazards on the job. However, a number of factors raise special concerns about working youth. Young workers typically work at a series of part-time, temporary, minimum-wage jobs, often going to their jobs after putting in the equivalent of a day of work at school. As new workers, young people are likely to be inexperienced and unfamiliar with many of the tasks required of them, unable to recognise workplace hazards, and unaware of their rights as workers. Many positive youthful traits such as energy, enthusiasm, and a need for increased challenges and responsibility, combined with a reluctance to ask questions or make demands of their employers, can result in young workers taking on tasks for which they are neither prepared nor capable of doing safely.

Youth have an awareness that if they cause trouble at work there is always a surplus of workers to replace them. This contributes to young people's reticence to refuse jobs and activities that might place them in danger. The level of physical development of young workers is also important to consider. Smaller workers may not be able to reach parts of machines and may lack the strength required for certain tasks designed to be carried out by adults. Larger youths may be given adult tasks simply because of their size without regard to their lack of experience and maturity.

Young workers are often employed in retail industries. Settings in which the exchange of money occurs are thought to be at an increased risk for workplace violence. Other risk factors that increase the dangers for youth working in these settings include working alone and working late in the evening and early morning—hours that fit many young people's schedules. Several U.S. reports suggest that young people generally do not receive adequate prevention training either in school or on the job. As they have little experience in the work force in general, they also do not recognise how much training may be necessary. Furthermore, many of the training materials that are available are not geared to youth.

Making Work Safer for Young Workers

As the workplace is made safer in general, it will be safer for young workers. At the same time, young workers deserve special attention and certain prevention efforts should be targeted specifically at young workers. These include:

— Eliminating hazards through redesign of the workplace or work processes in jobs commonly held by youth.

— Early orientation and instruction, preferably from the moment the young worker steps onto the worksite.

— Educating young workers, parents, employers, health providers, and school personnel about health and safety hazards and about workplace rights and responsibilities.

— Expanding the base of information about occupational injuries to guide prevention activities, including efforts to encourage the reporting of all incidents and injuries occurring to young people at work. This includes the reporting of even those accidents and injuries that do not lead to lost time.

— Emphasising to employers the importance of tailoring workplace policies to young workers. For example, there may be times when a "customer is always right" policy may be necessary in order to reduce the threat of violence.

— Extra observation of young workers by all supervisors and co-workers to protect the safety and well-being of new workers.

— How employers and supervisors can make work safer for young workers

— Know and comply with safety requirements that apply to your workplace. Post these requirements where workers can see and read them.

— Assess and eliminate the potential for injury and illness associated with tasks required of young workers.

— Provide comprehensive training to ensure young workers recognise hazards and are competent in safe work practices.

— Routinely check that young workers continue to recognise hazards and use safe work practices. Evaluate equipment that young workers might be required to operate to ensure that it is safe for their use.

— Ensure that young workers are appropriately supervised to prevent injuries and hazardous exposures. Involve supervisors and experienced workers in developing a workplace health and safety programme and in identifying and solving potential health and safety problems.

Young Workers Do

— Be aware that you have the right to work in a safe and healthy work environment free of recognised hazards and that you have the right to refuse unsafe work tasks and conditions.
— Remember that all workers, including young and part-time workers, are entitled to workers' compensation benefits in the event of a work-related injury or illness.
— Participate in all training programmes offered by your employer, or request training if none is offered.
— Recognise and be aware of the potential for injury at work and seek information about safe work procedures from employers.
— Identify the first aid attendant at your workplace.
— Locate the first aid kit at your workplace.
— Always use safety equipment and follow safe work practices.
— Preventing overexertion accidents

Reduction of Risk factors

The key to preventing injuries is to reduce or eliminate the risk factors contributing to the injuries. Workplace factors associated with overexertion accidents to the back include:

— Awkward back posture held for a period of time or repeated due to poor working heights and reaches. Examples include reaching for linen or supplies located on high shelves.

— Heavy or frequent lifting, pushing, pulling, and carrying. For example, lifting and carrying bulk food containers.

— Prolonged sitting or standing. Examples include:

1) Sitting—front office staff working on computers

2) Standing—a restaurant worker whose duties consist of greeting customers and working the cash

— Whole body vibration. For example, delivery truck drivers. The time to complete a task, how often it is repeated, and the worker's perception about time pressures can also influence workplace risk factors.

Reducing overexertion risks

Reducing risks need not be a complicated process. Following are examples of solutions in the hotel and restaurant industries:

— Store heavier or frequently used items at a height between workers' hips and chest to reduce awkward postures when handling these items. Place smaller loads in laundry washing machines to reduce tangling and the subsequent heavy pulling needed to remove the laundry from the washer.

— Use laundry carts with spring-loaded bottoms that rise as the cart is unloaded. This reduces repetitive, awkward bending.

— Install platforms at the base of laundry chutes to eliminate repetitive bending and lifting from the floor while sorting laundry.

— Use long-handled tools to reach the walls and tub when cleaning showers to decrease reaching and stooping. Ask a co-worker for help when moving heavy furniture. Employers should set a policy to give guidance in these situations.

— Ensure cleaning products and equipment are efficient and do not require extra force to use. For example, use a window cleaner that doesn't streak to reduce the number of wiping motions, or use a cleanser that removes dirt and grime with one swipe.

— Use smaller banquet trays to lighten loads and to make them easier to handle. Store clean plates on spring-loaded dollies to reduce repetitive bending.

— Use carts to move heavy products from storage coolers and freezers.

— Don't store heavy items in small, confined areas where the worker may not be able to use safe lifting techniques.

— Design or alter "pass through" windows in restaurants to reduce the risk of back injury. If they are too high or too deep, workers are forced to use long reaches and awkward postures to pick up orders.

— Lower storage racks at dishwasher stations to minimise awkward lifting and reaching. Lowering the racks or using a sturdy step stool can help to reduce the height of the lift.

— Add a footrest or matting to a hostess counter to give some relief from prolonged standing.

Reduce risks through organising work differently. For example, room attendants could unload laundry from their carts more often to lighten the loads they handle and to reduce the amount of pushing needed to move the cart. Train and supervise workers in safe work practices that have been developed to reduce their exposure to risk factors.

Preventing HIV/AIDS, and hepatitis B and C

Hotel and restaurant workers sometimes find used needles between bedsheets, under beds, in garbage containers, and hidden in washrooms. Sometimes cleaning staff come into contact with condoms when they try to unclog toilets. These items could be contaminated with blood and body fluids infected with tiny organisms that can cause disease in humans. These micro-organisms are known as bloodborne pathogens. The bloodborne pathogens of most concern are the human immunodeficiency virus (HIV) and the hepatitis B and C viruses. HIV causes the disease AIDS (acquired immune deficiency syndrome), and the hepatitis B and hepatitis C viruses cause diseases with the same names. Since exposure to blood and certain body fluids may spread these viruses, these diseases are also called bloodborne diseases.

Most hotel and restaurant workers won't ever contact, at work, blood and certain body fluids that can spread HIV and the hepatitis B and C viruses. But even employers and workers in settings where contact with blood and these body fluids is not expected should be aware of some basic precautions because it is possible to become infected with a single exposure incident—that is, harmful contact to infected blood and body fluids. This section provides information on the basic precautions that should be taken in such work settings.

Hepatitis B and C should not be confused with hepatitis A—a foodborne illness. That means that you can become infected with the hepatitis A virus if you eat food that has been prepared by someone who is infected with the virus. Hepatitis A is primarily a public health concern. Hotel and restaurant owners who would like more information on how to prevent the spread of hepatitis A should contact their local health units. How could someone be exposed to infected blood and body fluids at work? Workers can be exposed to infected blood and body fluids at work in the following ways:

— By puncturing the skin with sharp objects contaminated with infected blood and body fluids.

(Sharp objects are commonly known as sharps. These include needles, scalpels, knives, razors, scissors, broken glass, or anything that can pierce, puncture, or cut skin.)

— By splashing infected blood and body fluids into the tissues lining the eyes, nose, or mouth. These tissues are called mucous membranes.

— By splashing infected blood and body fluids on non-intact skin—that is, fresh open cuts, nicks, wounds, skin abrasions, chapped and damaged skin, and skin with diseases such as eczema and dermatitis.

Reduce the risk of infection

Where it is reasonable to expect that workers could be exposed to blood and certain body fluids as part of their normal job duties, employers must comply with the sections on biohazardous materials of the Occupational Health and Safety Regulation. Under these requirements, employers will typically have to develop and implement exposure control plans that eliminate or minimise the specific risks and hazards in their workplaces. Accident investigations are an important source of health and safety information. If a review of accident reports shows that exposure incidents involving blood and certain body fluids have occurred in the past, an exposure control plan may be required. There's a lot of concern in the workplace about HIV/AIDS, and hepatitis B and C. Even if contact is not likely to occur at a worksite, the employer can help allay such concern and can ensure that workers are prepared for unexpected events. To do this, employers should:

— Inform and instruct workers in how to eliminate or reduce the risk of contact with blood and certain body fluids

— Ensure that work practices eliminate or minimise the risk of unforeseen contact

— Develop ways to address chance encounters with blood and certain body fluids

— Provide workers with the equipment, tools, and personal protective equipment (PPE) needed to deal with an unforeseen contact

— Monitor the workplace to ensure that safeguards are used and safe work practices are followed. In case of an exposure incident, ensure that:

— Prompt, easy-to-access first aid and medical attention is available

— Employees are aware of procedures for obtaining immediate first aid and medical attention and for reporting incidents of exposure to blood and certain body fluids

— If an exposure incident occurs at the workplace, the employer must investigate it and, based on the findings, must develop ways to prevent similar incidents from occurring.

Safe Work Practices

Safe work practices explain how tasks are to be performed to reduce the likelihood of exposure to hazards. Even if workers aren't expected to be in contact with blood and certain body fluids, all workplaces should have basic safe work practices to deal with the rare incidents that could occur. The sample safe work practices in this section can be used to guide you in developing similar ones tailored to your workplace. Specific information about your workplace should be added, where relevant, or where it is needed to clarify instructions. Examples of the types of information that should be added include:

— Specific instructions on how to summon first aid and seek medical attention
— The person to report exposure incidents to
— What PPE (such as waterproof gloves) is required, when to use it, and how to obtain it
— The location of equipment and tools such as sharps containers, tongs, and spill kits

Handling pick up sharp

Don't pick up sharps and other items (for example, condoms) unless you have the appropriate equipment and PPE and you have been instructed how to do so safely. Don't pick up anything with the intention of discarding it later. For example, don't put a used needle in your pocket that isn't in a proper pocket container.

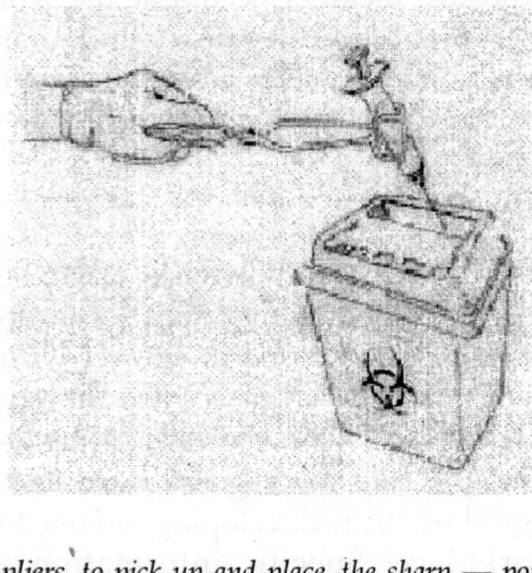

Use tongs or pliers to pick up and place the sharp — pointed end first — into the container

You could injure yourself before you discard it. Do not place needles in regular garbage under any circumstances—you may create a hazard for others. Follow these steps to pick up improperly discarded sharps and other items that could carry HIV and the hepatitis B and C viruses:

1. Wear disposable waterproof gloves (such as natural rubber latex, neoprene, nitrile, and vinyl), and have a proper sharps container and tongs or pliers ready.
2. Put the gloves on. Place the sharps container next to the needle or other item. Don't hold the container in your hand, or you might accidentally jab yourself.
3. If you are comfortable using tongs or pliers, use them to pick up the needle (or other item) and place it into the sharps container. This is the preferred method. If you are not comfortable using the tongs or pliers, pick up the needle by its shaft -with your gloved hand. In both cases, place the needle into the sharps container, pointed end first, away from you. Do not insert your fingers into the opening of the container, and keep your free hand out of the way.
4. Remove and discard the gloves. Wash your hands with soap and water.
5. Don't fill the sharps container to the brim. When it is about three-quarters full, replace it with a new one and properly dispose of the old one. Contact your municipality for information on disposal.

Removal of disposable gloves

Remove disposable gloves as soon as possible if they become damaged or contaminated. Remove them after you have completed the task that required gloves. Gloves should also be removed before leaving the work area. Do not wash and reuse your gloves. Use new gloves for each new task. Follow these steps to make sure your hands do not contact any blood or body fluids left on used gloves:

1. With both hands gloved:

— Grasp the outside of one glove at the top of the wrist.

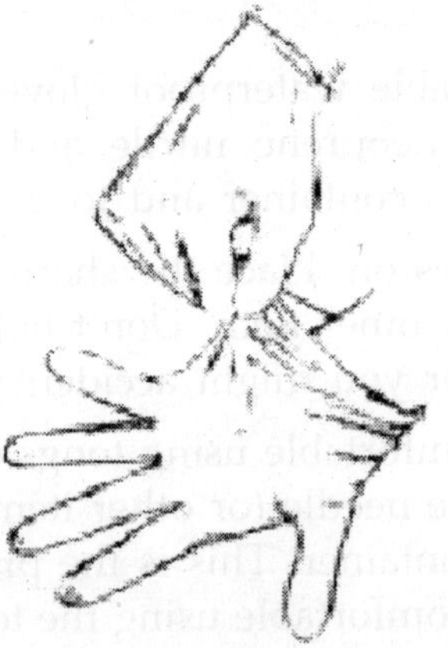

Grasp the outside of one glove

— Peel off this glove from wrist to fingertips while turning it inside out, as you pull the glove off your hand and away from you.

— Hold the glove you just removed in your gloved hand.

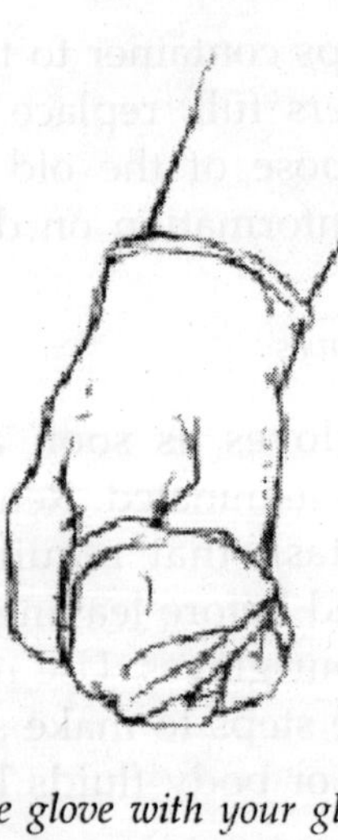

Hold the glove with your gloved hand

2. With the ungloved hand:

— Peel off the second glove by inserting your fingers on the inside at the top of your wrist.

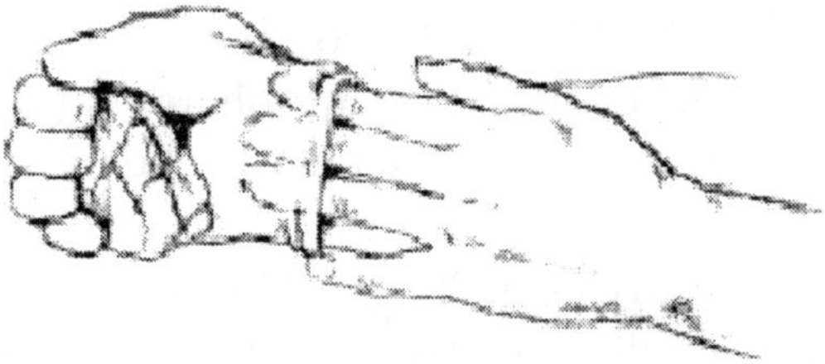

Insert your fingers on the inside of the glove

— Turn the glove inside out while pulling it away from you, leaving the first glove inside the second.

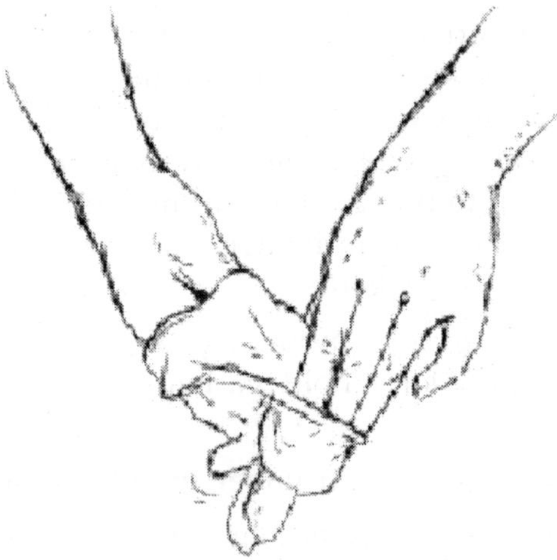

Turn the glove inside out over the first glove.

3. Dispose of the entire bundle promptly in a suitable waterproof garbage bag.
4. Wash your hands thoroughly with soap and water as soon as possible after removing gloves and before touching noncontaminated objects and surfaces.

How to handle garbage safely

Follow these steps to prevent contact with sharps and other items improperly discarded in garbage:

1. Handle garbage as little as possible.
2. Use waterproof garbage bags.
3. Be alert. If possible, look for sharps sticking out of the bags. Listen for broken glass when you move the bag.
4. Don't compress garbage or reach into garbage containers with your bare hands.
5. Don't use your bare hands to pick up garbage that has spilled out of an overflowing container. Wear puncture resistant and liquid-resistant gloves (the type worn by firefighters), or use other tools designed for picking up garbage.
6. Don't let garbage bags get too full, if possible. Leave enough free space at the top of the bag, so that when you grab it, you grab the top of the bag only—not any of the contents. You may have to change bags more often to prevent them from getting too full. This will also make them lighter—and thus easier to hold away from your body.
7. Hold garbage bags by the top of the bag, away from your body. Don't hold garbage bags against your body.
8. Don't place one hand under the bag to support it.
9. Dispose of wastes according to federal, provincial, and local regulations.

How to affect exposure incident

The following exposure incidents are potentially harmful:

— Skin is punctured with a contaminated sharp.

— A mucous membrane (the eyes, nose, or mouth) is splashed with blood and certain body fluids.

— Non-intact skin is splashed with blood and certain body fluids.

If any of the above incidents occurs, follow these steps:

1. Get first aid immediately

— If the mucous membranes of the eyes, nose, or mouth are affected, flush with lots of clean water at a sink or eyewash station.

— If there is a sharps injury, allow the wound to bleed freely. Then wash the area thoroughly with non-abrasive soap and water.

— If an area of non-intact skin is affected, wash the area thoroughly with non-abrasive soap and water.

2. Report the incident.

Report the incident as soon as possible to your supervisor and first aid attendant, or occupational health staff. This should not cause significant delay in seeking medical attention.

3. Seek medical attention immediately

Seek medical attention immediately—preferably within two hours—at the closest hospital emergency room, or at a health care facility if there's no hospital emergency room in the vicinity. Immunisations or medications may be necessary.

These may prevent infection or favourably alter the course of the disease if you do become infected. Blood tests should also be done at that time. You may need to see your family doctor within the next five days for follow-up, such as counselling and medications.

9

SAFEGUARDING THE GUESTS

The threats which a guest faces in hotels are seemingly unlimited. Certainly any threat common to the lodging industry and shown in the Protection Management Matrix may exist in the guest-room. The nature of each threat, the significance of it and the protection considerations against it will vary from property to property. There are, however, some protection considerations which are virtually universal and which should be incorporated into any guest protection countermeasures.

CRIMES AGAINST GUESTS

There are several problems related to crimes against guests that may call for separate analyses and responses. These are:

— prostitution;
— pickpocketing;
— confidence schemes (fraud);
— fencing of stolen property;
— organised crime and gang activities;
— offenses relating to casino gambling;
— crimes involving the elderly;

— burglary of holiday homes;
— robberies at bars and other businesses;
— terrorism against guests; and
— mass-transit crimes (e.g., at bus or airport terminals; on subways or trains).

Crimes Against Tourist Guests

Tourism is an interactive relationship among tourists, local businesses, and host governments and communities. Indeed, a long-established relationship exists between increases in crime and tourism; major economic crimes (e.g., robbery, burglary) in some highly popular tourism venues have a "similar season to tourism," for several reasons. First, tourists are lucrative targets, since they typically carry large sums of money and other valuables. Second, tourists are vulnerable because they are more likely to be relaxed and off guard-and sometimes careless-while on vacation. Finally, tourists are often less likely to report crimes or to testify against suspects, wishing to avoid problems or a return trip.

Tourist crimes generally involve one of several scenarios:

— The tourist is an accidental victim, in the wrong place at the wrong time, targeted as an easy mark.

— The location is conducive to crime, due to its nightlife, hedonistic culture, and myriad potential victims.

— The industry itself provides victims, as tourists are more prone to taking risks while on vacation, and less likely to observe safety precautions. Furthermore, as tourists' numbers grow, so too can local hostility toward tourists, thereby increasing the chances that they will be cheated, robbed, or assaulted.

— Terrorist or other groups may specifically target tourists, singling them out for hostage-taking or even murder.

Crimes against tourists can impede tourism by significantly damaging a location's image. Therefore, the most important prerequisite for a successful tourist industry is a reputation for having crime under control and guaranteeing tourists' safety. Furthermore, media coverage of crimes against tourists often tends to be out of proportion to the actual risk, having a profound effect on public perception of safety at particular locations.

Although theft is the most common crime against tourists, they are vulnerable to other crimes as well, including physical and sexual assault, credit card fraud, and scams. In areas with many adult entertainment venues, tourists tend to congregate and be disproportionately targeted by offenders. Furthermore, crimes against tourists tend to occur in areas with higher overall crime rates.

Tourists may unwittingly contribute to the problem through excesses and dangerous practices in sport and leisure activities, driving, gaming, and drinking-some of which is routine "vacation behaviour." They may also contribute to their victimisation by

— carrying and flashing large sums of money;
— visiting dangerous locations, or walking in isolated areas or dark alleys, especially at night;
— leaving valuable items in public view; and
— looking like a tourist (e.g., driving a rental car, carrying a backpack, carrying a camera, consulting a map, appearing lost).

Hotels, motels, downtown centres, shopping malls, bars, restaurants, tourist attractions, beaches, and airports are potential points of encounter for victims and offenders.

(Some communities have determined that the greatest number of tourist crimes occur when tourists leave airports and major highways, becoming lost in inner-city neighbourhoods.) Venues such as bars and nightclubs can encourage heavy drinking and a sense of freedom from normal constraints. Because tourists often are obvious by their dress, carry items easily disposed of once stolen, and are temporary visitors (and thus unable to put much pressure on police to act against criminals, or unlikely to appear as a prosecution witness), tourist zones allow pickpockets, swindlers, thieves, gang members, and robbers to commit crimes they might not otherwise attempt or be able to accomplish.

Tourist clustering also affords terrorists opportunities to commit acts against large numbers of people. Some tourist areas are also popular retirement areas, so the potential for crimes against the elderly increases significantly. The physical characteristics of tourist locations may also contribute to crime. For example, a visitor staying in an older motel with a dimly lit parking lot, and no private security officers or video monitoring, might be at risk. Moreover, tourist areas are characterised by anonymity and a high turnover of population, allowing offenders to conceal themselves, particularly when the police have to deal with massive increases in traffic volume and other routine work unrelated to crime.

In addition, many popular tourist locations are renowned for their scenic, isolated nature, inviting adventuresome tourists to explore remote surroundings. Tourists as Offenders It is worth noting that tourists may be the perpetrators, as well as the victims, of crime. The "tourist culture" can lessen tourists' sense of responsibility. They may riot at sporting events, for example, or cause disturbances on aircraft. They may also solicit prostitutes, buy illegal drugs, or smuggle goods out of the country. Furthermore, terrorists may pretend to be tourists.

Local Problems

Your agency's capacity to identify tourist-related incidents in its records management system is a major factor in being able to ask the right questions and develop proper responses. It would be helpful if a standard, international definition specified who a tourist is, what constitutes a crime against a tourist, and how tourist crime records should be kept. Then police departments in tourist areas could record and analyse tourist crimes separately, and thus better understand victimisation patterns.

You should review your agency's records management system to ensure there are uniform methods for reporting and classifying tourist crimes. Many tourist areas closely guard tourist crime data. To get an accurate picture of the problem, you may need to

— thoroughly review offence reports to identity touristrelated crimes (computer-aided dispatching systems may be coded to tabulate such crimes);

— conduct tourist surveys (e.g., through the local police, Chamber of Commerce, or hotels/motels) to determine the actual number of offenses; or

— encourage businesses-including hotels and motels-to report crimes or other problems concerning tourists to the police.

The following are some critical questions you should ask in analysing your particular tourist crime problem.

Incidents

— How many crimes (and what percentage of total crimes) in your jurisdiction involve tourists?

— What percentage of crimes are committed by tourists, as well as against them?

— What are the general circumstances surrounding the crimes (e.g., was a rental car involved, were the tourists lost)?

— What types and amounts of property are stolen, if any?

— What percentage of tourist crimes do you estimate are reported to the police?

— Do you suspect some false reporting of crime (e.g., to cover up the complainants' own wrongdoing or embarrassing acts)? If so, what percentage of reported offenses do you suspect are false?

Locations/Times

— Where do tourist crimes occur? Indoors or outdoors?

— In densely populated areas or remote areas? At repeat locations? In high-risk crime areas? Near major attractions?

— Where are tourists staying when the offenses occur (e.g., hotels, motels, private rental properties)?

— When do the crimes occur (day or night, day of week, time of year)? Victims

— Who are the victims (by gender, age, occupation)? Are there any noticeable demographic patterns among them?

— Where are they from? Are they regional, national, or international tourists?

— What percentage of victims are injured during the crimes? How serious are the injuries?

— How do they typically react to their victimisation? Are they cooperative with the police? Willing to stay or return to testify against the offender?

— What victim activities or attributes may have contributed to the crimes (e.g., drinking, flashing large sums of money, frequenting dangerous areas or exploring remote locations, having an alternative lifestyle)? Have they been careless about their personal safety and property?

— What percentage of attempted crimes have been thwarted by tourists or by other people? Offenders

— What are the offenders' demographics (age, gender, race, place of residence, and so forth)?

— Are they local, or from out of town?

— Do they appear to specialise in victimising tourists?

— Are they part of a loosely or formally organised group, or working alone?

— What are their motives (economic, political, personal)?

— What percentage of offenders commit crimes against tourists for money to buy drugs? What percentage either are or appear to be under the influence of drugs or alcohol during the offence?

— What percentage of offenders are repeat offenders?

— How prolific are the worst offenders?

— Do they use different techniques against tourists from those used in other crimes?

— What types of weapons do they use, or threaten to use?

Current Responses

— Do the police have a good working relationship with tourist-related businesses?

— Are funds provided to cover victims' travel expenses if they have to testify against offenders?

— Have police and private security employees been trained in crime prevention and reduction measures involving tourists?

— Is there a special police unit trained specifically to protect tourists and to assist tourism businesses with crime prevention measures?
— Are local citizens aware of the harm tourist crime can cause to the community, and of their role in preventing it?
— Are tourists informed about crime prevention measures (e.g., through brochures)?

Measures of the Effectiveness

Measurement allows you to determine to what degree your efforts have succeeded, and suggests how you might modify your responses if they are not producing the intended results. You should take measures of your problem before you implement responses, to determine how serious the problem is, and after you implement them, to determine whether they have been effective. Measurement will likely involve both quantitative (statistical) and qualitative (anecdotal) information. The following are potentially useful measures of the effectiveness of responses to tourist crimes:

— reduced numbers of offenses against tourists across the various offence types,
— reduced calls for tourist-related police service,
— reduced number and severity of injuries caused by crimes against tourists,
— reduced total average loss (both of cash and property) incurred by victims,
— increased tourist and local citizen perceptions of safety, and
— increased tourist reporting of crimes (for crimes against the person, you might compare emergency room records with police reports).

You should be alert to the possibility that your responses to tourist crime might displace it, either geographically, to other types of crime, or to non-tourist victims. You should also be aware that your responses to tourist crime might reduce non-tourist-related crime, as well.

Your analysis of your local problem should give you a better understanding of the factors contributing to it. Once you have analysed your local problem and established a baseline for measuring effectiveness, you should consider possible responses to the problem. The following response strategies are drawn from a variety of research studies and police problem-solving efforts; several of them may apply to your community's problem. It is critical that you tailor responses to local circumstances, and that you can justify each response based on reliable analysis.

In most cases, an effective strategy will involve implementing several different responses. Law enforcement responses alone are seldom effective in reducing or solving the problem. Do not limit yourself to considering what police can do; give careful consideration to who else in your community shares responsibility for the problem and can help police better respond to it. Unfortunately, there are few careful evaluations of tourist crime interventions. Much of what is recommended here is based on informed judgments about what is likely to be effective. General considerations for an effective strategy are:

1. Working with the tourism industry to identify and address crime-related concerns. Police representatives should participate on tourism boards and work with hotel/motel, convention, and visitors' bureaus to understand tourism-related problems and concerns, and to develop joint crime prevention programs. Police should provide ongoing information about local crime to tourism officials.

2. Training police and private security staff to recognise and address tourist-related safety concerns. Police and private security staff should know what particular crime risks tourists face, what resources are available, and how to access those resources (e.g., visitors' bureaus, emergency and social services, health departments). They should also be prepared to help tourists access emergency shelters, transportation systems, and foreign embassies, and help them navigate the various criminal justice processes.
3. Facilitating tourist victims' testimony in criminal cases. Tourist victims usually will not return to their vacation spots to give testimony, as it is costly and time-consuming: Hawaii has enacted, and other states have considered, statutes allowing crime victims to testify from their home via teleconferencing.
4. Imposing additional taxes in tourist areas to support special security measures. In some tourist areas, property owners pay a special fee to support security and other services that increase the area's appeal and reduce safety risks to tourists.
5. Encouraging hotels and motels to adopt practices that will reduce guest victimisation. Among the practices you should encourage are
   - requiring that guests show identification before reentering the building,
   - installing electronic room locks that are changed after each guest checks out,
   - providing safety deposit boxes,
   - installing surveillance cameras, and
   - employing full-time security officers. You might also encourage hotels and motels to provide safety tips on their website or in-house cable TV channel.

6. Offering rewards for information leading to the arrest and conviction of those who commit serious crimes against tourists. The tourism industry may be willing to help finance reward programs. In Miami, the local government developed such a program, in conjunction with Crime Stoppers and the tourist industry.
7. Educating tourists to reduce their risk of victimisation. Police in tourist areas should develop an array of methods for educating tourists about crime prevention. Among those you might consider are the following:
   - — creating a website with a dedicated tourist menu that
     - a) provides safety tips on such topics as rental and use of cars, and use of automated teller machines (ATMs), credit cards, and other financial instruments;
     - b) lists emergency telephone numbers;
     - c) has regularly updated tourist crime bulletins; and
     - d) provides information about any specialised tourist police or auxiliary patrols;
   - — equipping tourism officers with a cellular phone so they can quickly access information, translation services, or other assistance for tourists;
   - — establishing a 24-hour police information counter, installing "tourist telephones" (those specifically designated for tourists needing information and providing safety tips) and broadcasting precautionary messages at airports;
   - — establishing a tourist hotline for reporting crimes and related problems;
   - — encouraging positive media contacts regarding the tourist police program and tourist safety, including

having tourist officers take journalists on "ride-alongs";

— producing a video that provides information about the tourist area, the tourist police program, travel safety tips, and how to get around the area, for showing on inbound aircraft and in airports;

— providing information to foreign consulates and embassies, so they can educate their citizens about travel to your area; and

— developing a means to inform travellers of the safest places to stay (for example, some cities have a crime-free hotel/motel certification program that allows hotels/motels to qualify for special advertising based on their safety record).

The following are some common safety tips that particularly pertain to tourists:

— Use maps to plan routes before venturing out in a rental car.

— Avoid travelling in vehicles that are obviously rented.

— Avoid appearing to be a tourist.

— Be aware of surroundings and avoid suspicious characters.

— Travel with companions.

— Remove valuables from cars.

— Lock windows and doors in rooms when leaving. All tourist information should be available in the languages most commonly spoken by visitors to the area.

8. Increasing uniform patrols in tourist areas. Highly visible police patrols can discourage offenders who target tourists and increase tourists' sense of safety, but obviously, they are labour-intensive and therefore costly.

9. Deploying citizen patrols to supplement police patrols. Unpaid or paid citizen patrols during peak tourist seasons can supplement police presence. They can help inform tourists and discourage offenders. They should be conspicuously dressed, well informed about matters of concern to tourists, and have ready communication with police.
10. Conducting surveillance at high-risk locations. Surveillance should be based on local intelligence about problem areas and times. In general, surveillance is time-consuming and costly, and is effective at reducing crime only if it results in the apprehension of especially prolific offenders.
11. Changing the physical environment to reduce opportunities for tourist crimes. Such measures might include putting up appropriate signs for tourists at key locations (e.g., near airports) to prevent their becoming lost or a traffic hazard, or inadvertently going into high-risk areas.

Protecting Guest from Injuries

Guest injuries are common occurrences and result from a variety of hazards including, but not limited to, wet floors, worn carpets, exposed carpet tacks, broken furniture, electrical wires improperly laid along a floor, broken glass not vacuumed up, poor lighting, and lack of directions for equipment usage. The type of guest injury claim of greatest concern to security professionals is allegation of unsafe conditions based on the argument that the hotel had inadequate security protection. It is fair to say that this is a popular theory of liability now that the public is aware of the necessity for security protection in a hotel and lacks tolerance for levels of protection perceived as inadequate.

An innkeeper has the duty to exercise reasonable care for guests. If a hotel is experiencing an increase in crime, or if the surrounding neighbourhood is having problems with crime in a way that could affect the hotel's guests, the innkeeper must respond to that threat by improving or increasing security measures. If the innkeeper fails to do so, he or she may be liable for any injuries guests suffer at the hands of third-party criminals. Even if the offender is not caught, but the injury occurred in or immediately adjacent to the hotel's property, the hotel may be required to pay for damages.

Liability in these cases is predicated on the theory of negligence, in that it was reasonably foreseeable that the injury would occur if corrective action were not taken. If the innkeeper knew or should have known of the threat, the "reasonable care" rule will apply, establishing that the innkeeper had a duty to protect the guests, failed to do so, and as a result the guest was harmed. The objective of security should be "the protection of life and property". Therefore, the focus should be on preventing a loss in the first place. In view of this, the innkeeper, through her or his security department, must keep informed of recent trends or changes in crime patterns both within the hotel and in the surrounding neighbourhood.

A positive working relationship with the local police is essential for a regular flow of information regarding crime in the neighbourhood. The security department's reporting system should include both monthly and semi-annual reports that summarise all criminal activity for the time period covered and make everyone aware of emerging patterns of changes. There are no standards, the courts are making the determination of "adequacy" on a case-by-case basis.

Alcohol server liability arises when the server of alcoholic beverages is held liable for the actions of intoxicated persons who consumed alcoholic beverages in the liquor serving establishment, and as a result of the intoxication caused injury to themselves or another person. Alcohol liability problems generally do not involve security staff initially, for it is, usually food and beverage department employees such as bartenders, waitresses, and managers who are directly in control of and responsible for alcohol consumption.

Security does have a function to perform, however, in helping to prevent intoxicated patrons from driving a vehicle or becoming injured while walking around the hotel property. Not all alcohol liability cases are limited to motor vehicle accidents. Guests can become injured by falling down due to intoxication in an otherwise safe area. Unfortunately, in such cases the innkeeper is not able to claim the defence that it was the guest's intoxication that caused the injury, if it was the innkeeper who allowed the individual to get drunk in the first place. The greatest risk of alcohol liability arises when the guest attempts to leave the hotel and drive a car.

If a security officer is called for assistance in such circumstances, everything possible should be done to discourage the guest from driving. A hotel's management may even want to consider the extreme measures of refusing to return the guest's keys or calling the local police department. This action may cause other problems, but the hotel operator must weigh the risks and decide on the safest option.

Security frequently receives calls from bartenders who need assistance discontinuing service to a guest who, in the bartender's opinion, has had enough to drink. The security officer must respond promptly to such calls, for the situation is apt to get out of hand quickly. Once the security officer has arrived, she or he should obtain all relevant information from the bartender and, without question, back up the decision to discontinue service.

Security should never try to overrule the server's decision. The same rule applies to any member of management who is called in for assistance in such circumstances. For the subsequent report and follow-up investigation, it is essential to obtain all pertinent facts, names and addresses of witnesses, and documentation (e.g., bar tabs and statements) for future reference. All this information should be maintained in a file for at least the time of your state's statute of limitation.

Finally, it must always be remembered that reports, logs, and other documents are subject to legal review. The accuracy of each incident's facts is crucial to the hotel and its reputation. The security manager should consult with legal counsel and develop standard hold harmless agreements to be used by catering and convention service personnel. If the sales department is doing a thorough job, it will be able to conduct a group history, and hence be aware of any potential concerns during the actual booking of a convention. The security manager must be made aware of any potential groups that might have additional security needs.

Guest-room Protection

Confidentiality of the guest-room location is vital. No audible announcement of the guest's room number should be made at the front desk or at any location. When providing the key to the guest, he should be informed of the room number by the use of a card or key holder or some other nonverbal means. Obviously, when the bell staff is used, the room number again should never be verbalised but rather the bellperson should be informed of the room location in the same confidential manner by which the guest was notified. When receiving inquiries regarding a guest, whether by phone or in person, the confidentiality must again be maintained.

A guest's right to privacy is a vital and long-standing tenant of lodging and should never be violated. When a request is made for a room key by a person claiming to be an occupant of that room, positive identification must be made of that person prior to issuing a key. Standard identification methods should be established and used as appropriate. The locking system utilised at the guest-room door is a major consideration in this countermeasure. Basically systems available to the hotelier fall into one of four general categories. They are key in knob, standard mortise locks, mortise locks with programmable cylinders and/or removable cores, and electronic lock systems. Key-in-knob is a system in which the key channel is actually within and a part of the doorknob itself.

It is activated by inserting the key directly into the knob and the channel. This is probably the least effective of all systems, is considered generally insecure and in fact is prohibited in some states as a hotel/motel guest-room locking system. The word "mortise" means, literally, "a hole, groove or slot into or through which some other part of an arrangement of parts fits or passes". This system usually consists of a face plate, with the doorknob and an unconnected separate key channel on the exterior side of the door and a deadbolt arrangement on the interior side of the door.

Mortise locks with programmable cylinders and/or removable cores allow for quick key combination changes. Electronic lock systems allow for a unique selection of keying combinations whenever a new guest is assigned to that room, whenever a compromise or key loss is suspected and whenever management determines that such action is warranted. New and more sophisticated systems are reaching the market on a continuing basis and the choice for the hotelier is a difficult one. If there is a single rule-of-thumb to follow, it is that whatever system is chosen, it offers higher protection if the locking combination can be changed on a random or programmed basis whenever required.

Door and frame construction as well as attendant locking hardware should be of such quality and workmanship as to minimise the ease by which an intruder can bypass them by force. Obviously, the hinges should be located to preclude the pins being pulled from the exterior. Glass, either in the door or in a panel near the door, should be of such strength and of such configurations as to minimise the possibility of an intruder breaking it and reaching into the room and accessing the locking system. The lock bolt should be configured to minimise forceful entry and of such strength as to minimise being cut.

Self-closing automatic locking devices should be standard. Connecting room doors are those doors which are placed between guest-rooms to allow for access from one guest-room to another or to enlarge the rented space from one-room to two-or-more-room capacity. Historically, these doors often have been of lesser construction than the main guest-room door. In fact, the threat which is posed to the guest by inappropriate connecting room door design, maintenance or construction warrants special attention.

Single connection door arrangements are strongly discouraged. Instead, there should be two separate doors, each void of all hardware on the inside. In effect, then, there are two doors facing one another, neither with locking hardware and with space between them. On the guest-room side of each door, however, there should be provision for the guest himself to provide added self-protection. Only guests occupying both rooms simultaneously and in concert with one another or hotel/ motel staff should have the ability to access both rooms. View ports should be installed in the guest-room door.

The exception to this guideline would be in the case of those door/room configurations in which adjacent glass panelling allows observation of anyone immediately outside the guest-room door. A minimum 200-degree viewing angle is considered acceptable. A second view port for disabled persons is recommended and is in fact required in rooms complying with the Americans with Disabilities standards. Secondary and additional protective equipment is appropriate on the main guest-room door, depending on the locking system utilised.

Many door locking systems have a double locking dead bolt and single action panic release features installed within the system. Many states require the hotelier laws of that state to be posted prominently within the guest-room. The limits of liability in so far as the loss of personal belongings are normally shown and are posted so that the guest understands those limits. Also, normally noted on these postings are the considerations of safe deposit and property safekeeping facilities available at the property.

All too often, however it is the hotelier himself who has not kept his knowledge current. Announcements concerning what actions the guest ought to take in order to secure that door to the fullest extent possible should be posted on or near the back of the guest-room door. Use of the safety chain, if applicable, should be explained as should the use, if appropriate, of the dead bolt. All double locking procedures should likewise be explained. Use of the view port and methods of securing any connecting or sliding/patio doors should also be addressed. Personal injuries due to accidents occur more often in the bathroom than any other portion of the guest-room.

Postings, therefore, regarding tub safety, use of any grab bars, slip-and-fall deterrent bathmats, etc. should be considered. If particular use of electrical equipment in the bathroom is desired, warnings regarding their use should be posted. The guest-room telephone is more than a convenience. It can be, literally, a life-saving guest protection device. Consider posting prominently and distinctly on the phone faceplate a notation of the number to be called to summon help.

Of even greater concern, obviously, is the system devised to both answer immediately and prioritise any emergency calls. Several methods are possible to accomplish this immediate handling of any emergency call. The emergency number can be channelled, like all operator calls, into a central switchboard. If this is the system chosen, care should be taken that when the emergency number is dialled, it has an extremely distinct ring—much louder perhaps or with a distinct tone. Some hotel chains/ properties have adopted a procedure whereby the guest is advised to dial an outside number such as 911 to request emergency assistance. Great care and planning are essential before such a procedure is established.

Whatever method of immediate response is adopted, the recipient of the call, whether a front desk clerk, a switchboard operator or a security officer, must be trained and scripted in quick and accurate response. Many municipalities using the nearly universal 911 system have developed scripting which is quick and concise and makes misinterpretation or extraneous conversation of a minimal concern. The use of a warning light which is activated along with the distinct ring adds greater assurance that the operator will note the call immediately and cease all other duties to respond to it.

The emergency line might also be channelled into a continually manned security office, dispatch point or control centre. Again, the ringing apparatus and arrangement must be such that the ringing tone is clear, distinct and unique and is inevitably responded to immediately. Consideration should be given to installing a system so that the room number is displayed when a call is received. Automatic taping of the ensuing conversation is a plus. The lodging industry is long past the time when it was felt that education of guests about threats and dangers and protection methods were contrary to the "host image".

On the contrary, such announcements and notifications are now considered absolutely essential by most professional hoteliers. The bell staff should be scripted and instructed in all protection aspects of the guest-room. They should direct the guests to the TV announcement, if there is one, even turning the TV on and to the particular announcing channel so that the guest gets an early opportunity to view and hear it.

The bellperson should also call to the guest's attention the guest-room service directory and highlight the fact that there is a section regarding protection. Finally, the bellperson should mention the entire range of protection devices, techniques and announcements present in the room. He should discuss all subjects ranging from the use of the door devices, safe deposit system to advice about safety and fire protection.

Reasonable Care for Guests

Reasonable care is the hoteliers's duty to take sufficient reasonable care of his guests that they do not become victims of loss. For the most part, the hoteliers is not an insurer of the guest's safety. However, he is responsible for reasonable care of that guest, and in the absence of such care he may be held liable. If the failure to provide such care is proven and a guest suffers a loss, we can be held liable. With justification, many hoteliers complain that the courts demand reasonable care and yet seemingly have not issued a broad, quantifiable and measurable definition of it.

On one hand, the courts have required that we provide a specified level of care and warned that failure to provide that level can cause great financial liability. And yet on the other hand, the courts have not established easily definable benchmarks against which that attainment can be measured. As we examine this apparent quandary, we will discover why the contradiction exists and how we can and must solve it. Reasonable care is that level of care which a reasonable person has a right to expect under normal circumstances. Such a definition leaves much to circumstance and to subjectivity.

Such ambiguity has led to a tongue-in-cheek definition—reasonable care is what the jury decides it is. And perhaps this definition is more than just a flippant attempt to define the undefined. If the jury decides we did indeed provide reasonable care, then in fact we did provide it. Hoteliers should establish a guest protection programme which would convince any jury of their peers that such reasonable care was in effect. Such a scheme protects the guest, increases staff morale, impacts favourably on occupancy, convinces the court that we provide reasonable care.

The first step in developing such a scheme is clarifying some basic ground rules, keeping in mind our prime objective: to protect the guest in order to avoid liability. It is important to establish that there are certain elements within the law which must be proven before a judgment of liability against the hoteliers can be imposed. If the hoteliers is to be judged guilty of liability, following an incident involving a guest, the following elements must shown.

— The hoteliers had a duty to provide care to the guest, the incident was foreseeable.

— He failed to provide reasonable care.

— Failure to provide reasonable care caused the incident to the guest.

— The guest suffered a loss as a further result of the hoteliers's failure to provide such care.

The court will address and decide upon these elements. It is in our best interest to recognise and understand that of these five elements, the two which are most able to address are the foreseeability issue, and the question of reasonable car.

Foreseeability must be considered when determining liability. Unfortunately, the definition of foreseeability has been imprecise and almost entirely subjective. Broadly speaking, foreseeability, from a hotelier's standpoint, is that set of circumstances surrounding conditions about which the lodging manager had knowledge beforehand or of which he should have had knowledge. Stated another way, a judgment of liability requires a degree of foreseeability.

It requires that the event which occurred must have been foreseeable in the mind of the hoteliers. A no-liability judgment was rendered in the case of a random killing of patrons in a fast-food restaurant in San Diego because the act, in the judgment of the court, was so outrageous and so completely unpredictable as to be not foreseeable. Protection against the possibility of that act, then, was not a requirement of the owner. However, had similar crimes been in evidence—a history of drive-by shootings, for instance, the judgment might well have been otherwise.

Hoteliers can be held liable and suffer penalties if they fail to provide reasonable care, and a necessary ingredient in that verdict of liability is the fact of foreseeability. Was the hoteliers aware of risks involved, or by the same token, should he have been aware of such risks? Given these circumstances, it seems prudent for the knowledgeable and sophisticated hoteliers to begin his guest protection programme by determining the identity and severity of surrounding threats. While foreseeability determined from the hotelier's standpoint, the three factors enter into consideration are:

— Nature of the premises;

— Crime demographics; and

— Location.

These considerations are enumerated from the standpoint foreseeability of crime in any public access facility. McGoey postulates that when referring to expert testimony presented to a court that an established criterion for determining a level of crime foreseeability must be utilised in order to provide a sound basis for opinion testimony. No less is true for the hoteliers establishing and maintaining his guest protection programme. He must have a criterion from which to build his protection profile. That criteria will allow for a complete analysis, the results of which will identify a level of crime foreseeability, which can be used to evaluate the adequacy of an existing security programme on a premises.

Nature of the premises is the first and most important factor of foreseeability. If the premise in question is a jewellery store, the foreseeability of armed robbers is more likely to be higher than the foreseeability of the crime of obscene phone calls, irrespective of the seriousness of the crimes being compared. By the same logic, the type of establishment within the same grouping impacts on the foreseeability of the type crime in question.

For instance, the likelihood that the crime of room theft in a hotel would occur is, obviously, higher than that of embezzlement. A hotel which has a high-energy lounge, caters to a younger crowd and demands a higher percentage of return on liquor sales could expect more and different crime problems than a property catering to a retirement-aged clientele. Not only the type of premises by the use thereof will have an influence on foreseeability.

Considerations include hours of operation, types of products and services offered, classification of clientele, age and experience of staff as well as the size, age and design of the property itself. These are but some of the considerations to be examined and analysed by the general manger and the Protection Management Committee. Crime demographics are elements involved in evaluating previous crime are a determination of which crime classifications are relevant, the relevant radius around the incident, the proper time frame, the type and precision of data available, and an estimate of the proportion of crimes that are officially documented.

These considerations, when viewed collectively and in concert with one another provide a basis for foreseeability determination that is much more accurate and useful than simply raw numbers. There are many factors which can skew data and distort reality. These are:

— Many crimes go unreported by the victims.

— Crimes which occur to a victim on a public premise often go unreported by the premises.

— Official crime statistics are grouped geographically into boundary segments or census tracts, which may or may not accurately reflect those statistics relative to the subject property.

— Crime categories are often not reflective of the crime itself.

— It is not uncommon for reporting agencies to either under- or over-report crime for their own purposes.

Low reporting might show police agency success or high reporting might indicate a means of justifying added staff. Therefore, it becomes patently obvious that raw crime data used to the exclusion of other related data is greatly suspect and invites incorrect analysis. The location is the least substantial. Its relative importance is generally subject to what has been found through investigation of the other two factors. It is the most likely to be influenced by physical conditions such as fences, foliage, signs, etc., and procedural conditions such as locking schedules, security patrol methods and incident reporting systems.

All crime types are not foreseeable everywhere. A rapist who gained access through a fourth floor exterior window of a high-rise apartment by using superior mountain climbing skill would not be reasonably anticipated and therefore not normally foreseeable. However, a recently constructed 24-hour convenience store in the centre of the highest crime zone in the city should anticipate a variety of property and personal crimes because of its location alone. Its level of crime foreseeability should be considered as potentially moderate to high from opening day. Its actual level and type of crime foreseeability will be modified later and affected by the actual nature of the business and its ability to control criminal activity through use of security techniques.

Safety Deposit Boxes

Every hotels are either using in-room safes for securing guest valuables or even foregoing having safety deposit boxes available for guest use at all. This is creating some confusion as to how to take advantage of the protection hotels enjoy under Innkeeper's Law regarding the loss of guest valuables. In spite of the availability of the in-room safes, a hotel must continue to accept and deposit valuables and to be prepared to, "give the guest a receipt for them" (the valuables). In other words, a guest who loses his or her property in the guest room, whether they use the in-room safe or not, has a claim against the hotel if the hotel does not comply with all the details of the law.

At some hotels with in-room safes, as part of the registration process, guests are asked to initial a stamped area on the registration card without explaining its significance. This stamp explains briefly something about the in-room safes and a dollar key charge or deposit. The hotel then adds a $1.00 per night charge for the in-room safe to the guest's folio. The typical guest would not carefully read or understood what they are initialing. The initials are the vehicle by which these hotels obtain the guest's authorisation for the daily charge.

These hotels are sometimes instructing their front office staff to tell the guests that the $1.00 is "security insurance". The term "insurance" has a very specific meaning and the application of this $1.00 charge for the availability of the in-room safes is probably not related to any real insurance policy. To say these safes are covered by insurance, if they are not, is misleading. To insure that the use of safety deposit boxes, in those hotels that have them, is adequately controlled, here are a few ideas to consider:

— File the box record (signature cards) with guest folios rather than in separate file. This will cut down on guests checking out and forgetting they have a box. It also insures that only guests and employees have boxes.

— File employees' box records with their personnel records. The General Manager or Controller should keep a current list of what boxes are assigned to employees.

— Keys for unused boxes should be kept in the Front Office Cash drawer or some other locked place, not in the key holes.

— Two or three employee safe boxes should be pulled and counted each month on a surprise basis to insure the boxes are correct and that no unauthorised items are in the box.

— Guests should be given privacy or a discreet distance when they are placing or removing articles from their box.

— If your hotel has in-room safes that you maintain a few safety deposit boxes at the front desk so, that in addition to posting the law properly, you will have fully complied with the Innkeeper's Law.

Customer Relationship Management (CRM)

The most typical approach to CRM has hotels developing point solutions, something that solves one particular problem, out of acute necessity. However, whether you use a consulting firm to help you implement the point solution or you go it alone, you should be sure that the key questions around direction, integration, processes and people are being asked. Generally speaking, the questions are a lot more easily asked than answered, which leads most companies back to the need for an overarching strategy and the realisation that CRM really is a way of running the business, not just the program du jour. Additionally, CRM is a way to increase revenues and/or reduce costs. Not understanding the fact that this is a bottom line strategy could lead you to make the wrong decisions in establishing your strategy.

Towards Effective CRM

Everyone wants to be a CRM Hero — the desired outcome. No one wants to be a CRM Zero — the career-limiting option. A few words of advice are given below.

CRM is very-much technology-based. A CRM Hero must demonstrate the leadership necessary to develop a CRM strategy and get the rest of the company to come along for the ride. At the risk of stating the obvious, too many hotels have adroitly demonstrated that they have no clue where their CRM program is going – but, wow, look at all that data! Never mind that they will soon be another case study in failed expectations. However, with a well-conceived strategy that highlights all aspects of the customer relationship, they would be able to clearly articulate the specific changes, tools and techniques that must be employed over time within their organisation to deliver measurable results.

Communicating the strategy to the rest of the people in the hotel the guests is very important. Not much new technology is needed for this step, either. However, you are guaranteed to fall short of your CRM goals without effective communication throughout the company. Meanwhile, the CRM Hero grows ever more frustrated that people don't "get it." Yet, people are the most vital, and the most frequently overlooked, part of the equation. If people don't understand the importance we are suddenly placing on effective relations with the guests, those relations will be anything but effective.

Successful CRM Implementations

Keep It Simple, Stupid (K.I.S.S.) Principle

There are a few home truths about successful CRM implementations. The K.I.S.S. principle is highly applicable. Over-complicating the process does one thing – it succeeds in extending the duration, potentially causing budgetary over-runs. In the words of Dr. Chekitan Dev, associate professor of strategic marketing at Cornell University's School of Hotel Administration, "Do not draw up a long-winded program. It is important to have quick hits that show short-term benefits – this will help to get people on board, since they want to see results. Maintain the built-in potential to upgrade... a simple process that grows organically will be the most successful, and yield the best results." If you must plan a gargantuan CRM program, "break it down into shorter-term, focused projects with clearly defined business benefits and success metrics".

Actionable measurements and performance metrics

It is important to ensure that adequate emphasis is placed on establishing timely and actionable measurements. It is crucial to be able to identify the bottom line impact on an ongoing basis of the program that has been established.

Stakeholder ownership

If you want to ensure a successful implementation, it is important to ensure that all stakeholders are on board. It is not merely sufficient if key players buy into the process. They must take ownership of, and be actively engaged in the process.

GIGO

Better known as "Garbage In – Garbage Out," this is the test of stakeholder ownership. Realize that none of the exciting new capabilities are worth anything without good data. In our experience, legacy systems generally have errors in roughly half of their customer records. These could be as simple as an address that reads "road" instead of "street," or as complicated as multiple customer records for the same customer, each with slight differences. Yet you have countless opportunities to capture good data in the course of a guest experience. Part of your business process work has to be to ensure effective capture and cleansing of customer data. Effective capture implies not sticking all of the good stuff in the comments field, where it likely resides today, completely unread in the hustle and bustle of the typical front desk.

Consider the value of the customer

Successful CRM is not about providing the best service on the block; rather, the key to effective relations with your customers is in providing appropriate service. We all know that customers are not equal. That's why loyalty programs were invented. Yet far too frequently we see clients that developed sophisticated segmentation capabilities and tiered loyalty programs who have no means of differentiating the service they provide to these segments of guests.

One resort client was excited about his newfound ability to execute real-time marketing campaigns to fill short-term availabilities at the hugely popular property. Yet he had not considered the value associated with different customer segments and was disappointed when the realisation from these last-minute guests was not up to the usual standards of the resort. Simply put, this client was ignoring all of its segmentation data and mass-marketing its limited capacity. Thus, it is important to provide appropriate service at every interaction based upon intelligent segmentation.

Help your employees help your guests

All employees, at all properties, should have the training and up-to-date information that allows them to provide seamless, consistent, personalised service to the customer. According to Jens Thraenhart, director Internet strategy, Fairmont Hotels and Resorts, "A successful CRM and customer retention strategy in the hotel industry is dependent on the implementation at the property level. It is important to train front line employees to capture information from many offline touch points, in combination with online data capture. Training is vital to ensure consistency and cleanliness of guest information."

This information should be immediately available to front desk receptionists, call center agents, pit bosses, concierge and housekeeping staff, and so on, and should be served up at the right time.

This is where the true test of CRM solutions takes place. There is nothing worse for your relationships than raising expectations and then failing to meet them.

— Does the call center know about the e-mail campaign that marketing just sent out?

— Does the front desk recognise that the repeat guest standing before them remembers the way to the elevator and doesn't need a 60-second refresher course complete with maps?

— Does the reservations agent realise that the potential guest on the telephone has used the onsite spa the past three times she has been at the property, and might just want to get services booked in advance? And doesn't want to be transferred to the spa to start over with names, dates and addresses?

Truly successful CRM implementations anticipate these kinds of issues and build the requisite business processes, employee training and integrated systems necessary to meet or even exceed growing expectations.

10

Occupational Health and Safety in Workplace

Tourism and hospitality are service industries; as such, their people are crucial to their business success. A commitment to health and safety in the workplace makes good business sense because it is one way for a business to protect its greatest resource—its people. Such a commitment can:

— Create better work environments

— Increase worker participation in decision making

— Boost morale

— Help businesses retain good workers

— Improve productivity and enhance customer service

In addition, workplace accidents can take a great toll on workers, their co-workers, and their families, in terms of pain and suffering, disability, stress, and loss or change of employment. For a small business, such accidents can also be financially devastating.

Management of Health and Safety

The keys to managing health and safety in your hospitality business are a series of steps to prevent accidents and injuries from occurring. You need to know the hazards and risks, consider how they may affect workers, and determine what you can do to control them. The key steps include:

— Identification of hazards and assessment of risks, so you can focus on those things that are most likely to cause accidents

— Safe work procedures, which spell out how work is to be done safely

— Orientation, education, training, and supervision, which are particularly important for young workers and new workers

— Safety inspections to identify workplace hazards so that they can be eliminated or controlled

— Investigation of accidents and incidents, to find out why they occurred so that the causes can be corrected

— Regular health and safety meetings with your workers, where supervisors and workers can raise any concerns about health and safety

— Provision of first aid, which can reduce the severity of injuries

— Keeping records and statistics, which can help you identify recurring problems and ensure that hazardous conditions are being corrected Together these steps make up a health and safety programme.

Programmes for Health and Safety

All workplaces are required to have an Occupational Health and Safety Programme. There are two general types of programmes, formal and less formal (or informal). Formal programmes are required in hospitality businesses with 50 or more workers. Once you have developed processes to improve worker health and safety, it is important to review them at least once a year to make sure they address current concerns.

Risks Assessments in Workplace Hazards

You can prevent most workplace injuries and illnesses if you identify workplace hazards and eliminate or minimise the risks from them. Ways to minimise the risks include:

— Modifying work processes or equipment (for example, evaluate safety features when purchasing or replacing equipment)

— Developing and implementing safe work procedures

— Ensuring that appropriate personal protective equipment (PPE) is used and safe work procedures are followed:

Overexertion

More than a quarter of overexertion accidents in hotels and motels result from moving fixtures and furniture. Use proper lifting techniques:

— Place feet apart for good balance.

— Bend knees.

— Keep load close to centre of body.

— Use smooth, gradual motions.

— Avoid twisting your back.

Burns

About 16% of accidents in restaurants result in burns and scalds. Spilling or splashing of hot liquids and contact with hot surfaces are the most common causes. To reduce the risk of burns and scalds:

— Dry items thoroughly before using with hot oil.

— Slowly lower food and utensils into hot oil.

- Make sure handles of pots and pans do not stick out from counters or stoves.
- Use oven mitts or dry cloths when handling hot objects.
- Open lids away from you to allow steam to escape.

Guarding

Common equipment such as mixers, meat slicers, general maintenance equipment, and electrical tools can cause serious injuries during operation. Guarding, when used properly, can protect workers from serious cuts, crushing injuries, fractures, and amputations. To reduce the risk of injury:

- Make sure all guards are in place before using equipment.
- Check manufacturers' instructions on safe use.
- Retrofit older equipment with guards whenever possible.

Lockout

Equipment that starts up unexpectedly, especially during cleanup or maintenance, can cause many serious injuries. To reduce the risk of injury, unplug equipment before doing clean-up, maintenance, or repairs. If the equipment is hardwired, follow the specific lockout procedure for that equipment.

Cuts

Knives are involved in many accidents in the hospitality industry, especially among chefs and cooks. Injuries range from minor cuts to loss of fingers. To reduce the risk of injury:

— Use a flat surface or cutting board.
— Use the right knife for the job and make sure it is sharp.
— Hold the knife securely with your stronger hand.
— Curl the fingers of the other hand over the object to be cut.
— Cut away from your body when cutting, trimming, or deboning.
— Wear protective equipment such as cut-resistant gloves if *necessary*.

Slippery surfaces

Slippery surfaces are one of the major causes of accidents in the hospitality industry. To reduce the risk of this type of accident:

— Use non-slip footwear.
— Keep floors free from water or grease.
— Clean floors regularly.
— Clean up spills immediately.
— Put up warning signs around spills or wet floors.
— Consider installing non-slip tiling or other non-slip floor products.
— Use rubber mats in areas where the floors are constantly wet.
— Use slip-resistant waxes to polish and treat floors.

Occupational Health and Safety Regulation

The Occupational Health and Safety Regulation describes the minimum requirements to deal with specific hazards and prevent accidents and injuries. It applies to employers and workers in all workplaces.

Procedures for Safe Work

Some tasks require that a specific safe work procedure be followed to eliminate or minimise risks. For example, in your workplace you may have developed a procedure for operating equipment, clean-up, cash handling, or disposing of hot oil. Not all tasks require a written procedure. In deciding whether or not a written procedure is required, consider the following:

— How severe would the consequences of an accident be?

— How often is the task done?

— How complex is the task?

In general, safe work procedures are written for:

— Hazardous tasks

— Complicated tasks, so that important steps don't get missed

— Frequently performed tasks

Less routine tasks if reminders are needed about the hazards and the safe way to do things For certain tasks, a written procedure may not be necessary and safety issues can be addressed verbally when training the worker. The written procedures must list any required personal protective equipment, when it must be used, and where it can be found. Post the procedures prominently at the locations where the tasks are performed or next to the equipment used for the tasks.

Supervisors and managers will find them helpful in training workers how to do their jobs safely. Workers are then responsible for following these procedures. Examples of tasks in the hospitality industry where you may find that you should provide written safe work procedures include:

— Disposing of hot oil
— Handling of garbage
— Cleaning of blood and body fluids
— Cleaning of bathrooms, ovens, or swimming pools
— Turning of mattresses

The Occupational Health and Safety Regulation requires written procedures for some specific tasks or situations. Examples common to most hospitality small businesses include:

— Lockout
— Workplace violence
— Working alone
— Chemical spills
— Clean-up of biological materials
— Emergency evacuation.

Development of Safe Work Procedure

The process of developing a written safe work procedure involves the following:

— Determining the overall task for which the safe work procedure is needed
— Breaking down this overall task into its basic steps
— Identifying the hazards associated with each basic step
— Identifying actions to minimise the risks to workers from these hazards

These actions that workers must do when performing the task As an example, let's take a look at developing a safe work procedure for one very common and very hazardous activity in kitchens—cleaning the deep fat fryer. The overall task can be stated as follows: drain the oil from the deep fat fryer and transfer it into the oil dump drum for disposal.

The basic steps are:

— Draining the oil from the deep fat fryer into a container

— Transporting the oil through the kitchen and out to the oil dump drum

— Transferring the oil from the container into the oil dump drum

Workers of all ages face hazards on the job, but a number of factors raise special concerns about young workers, those aged 15 to 24. Young male workers in this age group are at a greater risk of being injured than any other age group. Over half the accidents involving young workers occur within the first six months on the job. This may be because:

— They are often new to a job

— They have less experience in recognising hazardous situations

They may be more reluctant to ask questions or raise safety concerns A large number of young workers are employed in the hospitality industry. It is important to discuss safety topics during any on-the-job training to help them recognize the importance of safety on the job.

Safety Orientation and Education

When you hire new and young workers, it's important to give them a safety orientation to the worksite on the first day of work, before they start working. This is because a worker's risk of suffering a work-related injury is greatest during the first six months on the job.

During the orientation:

— Explain that the worker should not be performing any task that the worker is not trained to do safely.

— Encourage the new worker to ask questions whenever the worker is unsure of anything.
— Introduce the new worker to the worker health and safety representative or safety committee member, if any.
— Explain the following to the worker:
  1) Potential hazards on the job, such as hazardous materials or electrical equipment
  2) Their responsibilities, and any restrictions on their activities
  3) How to report potential hazards and unsafe work conditions
  4) How to get first aid
  5) How to report injuries and accidents
  6) Location of emergency exits, and rescue and evacuation procedures.

Training for workers

All workers need supervised, hands-on training in how to safely perform their tasks before they start the job. Properly trained workers can have a positive impact on your business's productivity and service. Here's a general procedure that supervisors can follow when training new and young workers.

Prepare the new worker:

— Explain the job in detail, including any safety precautions or personal protective equipment required.
— Encourage questions from the worker and take the time to answer them fully.

Train the new worker

— Demonstrate and describe the procedure, including all safety precautions.

— Go through the procedure at normal speed, then at slow speed while the worker asks questions.
— Have the worker perform the procedure until he or she can do it exactly as required.
— Answer any questions or repeat any key points the worker may have missed.
— Keep written records of training, documenting who, what, and when.

Check and observe the new worker on the job

— Monitor the worker to ensure that safety standards are maintained.
— Make unscheduled visits.
— Correct unsafe work habits.
— Reinforce and recognise good work habits.

Supervision

Young workers in hotels and restaurants may find themselves in a situation where they supervise their co-workers even if they don't have the title of supervisor or assistant manager. Often they may not realise all the implications of this supervisory role, especially with regard to health and safety. As a supervisor, you're responsible for ensuring the health and safety of those whom you supervise. Your responsibilities include:

— Explaining the hazards of the job
— Instructing new workers in safe work procedures
— Ensuring that workers have been trained for all tasks assigned to them, including all safety precautions and safe work procedures
— Ensuring that any safety equipment and personal protective equipment is maintained and in good working order

— Ensuring that all materials are properly stored and handled
— Enforcing health and safety requirements
— Correcting unsafe acts or conditions that you observe or that workers bring to your attention
— Continually monitoring worker performance and well-being
— Setting a good example in following safe work procedures, using personal protective equipment, etc.

Safety inspections

— Inspect your workplace regularly.
— Besides correcting any hazards that you observe from day to day, set aside time for regular workplace inspections, and then eliminate or control any hazards found. Inspection is an ongoing task because the workplace is always changing. It is far better—and less costly—to prevent accidents than to deal with their consequences. Because safety inspections are preventive in nature, they are an important part of your overall health and safety programme.

You need to inspect your workplace often enough to prevent unsafe working conditions from developing. In hospitality small businesses this is typically once a month. You also need to inspect/assess your workplace when you've added a new process or when there has been an accident. Inspections should be conducted by a supervisor and a worker. If possible, the worker health and safety representative or members of the joint health and safety committee should be involved.

How to inspect

During an inspection:

— Use a checklist to ensure that your inspection is both thorough and consistent with previous inspections.

— Ask yourself what hazards are associated with the job that you are observing or that would be performed at that work area.

— Check how work is being performed. Are safe work procedures being followed? Is personal protective equipment being used?

— Talk to workers about what they're doing. Ask about safety concerns.

— Ask workers how they perform their tasks.

— Record any unsafe actions or conditions that you observe.

There are different ways of approaching safety inspections, depending on the objectives of your health and safety programme. For example, you can focus on the most common tasks performed by workers, or you can focus on a specific issue addressed by your programme, such as ergonomics.

The following are some examples of things to look for:

— Improper storage of materials, for example, in front of emergency exits or electrical panels, or blocking aisles or stairs

— Accumulation of liquid or grease on floors

— Failure to put a sign or barrier near wet floors

— Dull knives

— Lack of guarding on mixers and other equipment

— Lack of visibility through swing doors

— Poor maintenance of dollies, carts, etc.

Check whether safe work procedures are being followed.

For example:

— Is the meat slicer unplugged while being cleaned?

— Are gloves being used for handling garbage?

— Are proper lifting procedures being used?

— Do workers know the procedures for working alone?

Action taking

Remedy serious hazards or unsafe work practices immediately. For example, if you find that a ladder has a loose or damaged rung, immediately remove it from service and repair it or replace it with a new ladder. Classify other hazards according to priority and assign someone to remedy each. Follow up on any action that will need time to complete.

— Communicate your findings to the workers.

— Investigating accidents and other incidents

— Promptly investigate all accidents and near misses.

— Accidents are preventable, and when they happen they must be investigated. The goal is to find out what caused the accident and correct the causes so that other workers will not be injured in a similar way.

— Everyone in the business has a role to play in this:

— Workers must report accidents and incidents to their supervisors.

— The owner, employer, or supervisor must promptly start investigations of accidents and incidents.

— If possible, one employer representative and one worker representative should participate in the investigation.

Determination of investigation

The investigation should determine:

— Who was involved or injured?
— Where did the accident happen?
— When did it occur?
— What were the immediate and contributory causes?
— Why was the unsafe act or condition allowed?
— How can a similar accident be prevented?

To conduct an accident investigation, you need to identify any unsafe conditions, acts, or procedures that contributed to the accident. Consider the following:

— Unsafe or defective equipment
— Unsafe environment or conditions
— Poor housekeeping
— Physical hazards
— Poor planning
— Poor instruction
— Unsafe work practices
— Unusual or unfamiliar work conditions
— Personal factors

Interview witnesses and the people involved in the accident or incident, even if they weren't present at the accident or incident. For example, it may be appropriate to interview a supervisor who gave instructions at the start of the shift, or a trainer who instructed the workers involved months earlier.

Preventing Accidents

— Regular health and safety meetings
— Hold regular monthly meetings with workers to discuss health and safety matters.

You probably have regular discussions with workers to deal with production, marketing, daily specials, and other aspects of your business. Such discussions need not be very long—a few minutes at the beginning of a shift or some other appropriate time might be sufficient. It makes good business sense to show the same kind of commitment to health and safety.

Good communication is key to risk reduction and injury prevention. Regular monthly meetings are an important means of communication between supervisors and workers. The intent of these regular meetings is to maintain cooperative interest in health and safety in the workplace. Health and safety meetings need not always be formal or very long, but workers should feel free to bring up any concerns they may have. A record of each meeting should be kept and posted for everyone to read. A list of health and safety action items should come out of the meeting.

In workplaces with more than 9 and fewer than 20 employees, a worker health and safety representative is required. These representatives act as advisors and work cooperatively with employers and workers to identify and resolve workplace health and safety issues. During health and safety meetings, the worker health and safety representatives should raise any issues that workers brought to their attention since the last meeting. Workplaces with 20 or more regular employees must have a joint health and safety committee. This committee must have regular monthly meetings. The committee must have both worker and employer representatives.

First aid

Good first aid treatment can reduce the severity of work-related injuries, thereby minimising the financial costs associated with extensive medical treatment or the need to replace employees who are unable to work. All hospitality small businesses need to keep a first aid kit onsite. The type of kit and the need for a first aid attendant will depend on the number of workers and the travel time to the nearest hospital. Most hospitality small businesses require only a basic first aid kit, which includes such items as bandages, scissors, and latex gloves. Keep a record of all workplace injuries or diseases on file. Use the following chart to determine your first aid requirements.

Every worker must be made aware of where the first aid kit is located and how to call the first aid attendant if one is required. If a first aid attendant (FAA) is required, that attendant must hold a first aid certificate of the level necessary for that workplace. Post signs in your workplace indicating how to access first aid.

Transportation

Your business needs written procedures for transporting injured workers. Post these procedures in your workplace. These procedures should include:

— Who to call for transportation

— How to call for transportation

Prearranged routes in and out of the workplace and to the hospital Employers are responsible for the cost of transporting an injured worker from the workplace to the nearest source of medical treatment.

Keep Records and statistics

Keep all your health and safety records on file. Just as you keep files on other aspects of your business, so you should keep records and statistics on its health and safety performance. This should not be seen as a burden but as something that will contribute to the success of your business by helping prevent accidents and injuries in the workplace.

Orientation, education, and training records can help you ensure that all workers are getting the education and training they need. They can also help you determine how these factors are influencing your workplace health and safety performance. Accident and incident reports can tell you what hazards have caused accidents and incidents and what has been done to eliminate them.

Meeting records can help you monitor how promptly and how well "action items" have been carried out. First aid records can provide information about the numbers, types, and severity of injuries at your workplace so you can prioritise your health and safety efforts.

Statistics that may be of value include:

— How many incidents and injuries occur each year?

— How many work days are lost each year?

— What was the cost to your business from workplace injuries each year?

Through these actions, employers can demonstrate their commitment to taking all reasonable care to protect the wellbeing of their workers—their greatest resource.

Workers' role

— Take reasonable care to protect your health and safety and the health and safety of other persons who may be affected by what you do or don't do.

— Comply with the Occupational Health and Safety Regulation and other legal requirements.

— Follow established safe work procedures.

— Use the required personal protective equipment.

— Refrain from horseplay or similar conduct that may endanger others.

— Ensure that your ability to work safely is not impaired by drugs, alcohol, etc.

— Report accidents and incidents to your supervisor.

— Report to your supervisor or employer any hazard that might endanger others, any problem with protective equipment or clothing, or any violation of the Regulation and other legal requirements that you are aware of.

— Cooperate with your worker health and safety representative or joint health and safety committee.

Role of supervisors

— Ensure the health and safety of all workers under your direct supervision.

— Know the requirements of the Regulation that apply to the work you are supervising.

— Ensure that workers under your direct supervision are informed about all safety hazards in the workplace and that workers comply with the Regulation.

— Consult and cooperate with the worker health and safety representative or joint health and safety committee.

Role of employers

— Ensure the health and safety of your workers.

— Remedy any workplace conditions that are hazardous to your workers' health and safety.

— Ensure that your workers are informed about all safety hazards in the workplace, comply with the Regulation, and know their rights and duties under the Regulation.

— Establish occupational health and safety programmes as required.

— Provide and maintain protective devices, equipment, and clothing, and ensure that workers use them.

— Provide your workers with the education, supervision, and training necessary to ensure that they do their work safely.

Safe Use of Cleaning Chemicals

There are many different types of hazardous cleaning chemicals are used in the hospitality industry. They include washing-up liquids, dishwasher detergents and rinseaids, drain-cleaning products, oven cleaners, disinfectants, toilet cleaners, bleach, sanitisers and descalers. The most common risks are likely to be through contact with the skin or eyes, breathing in or swallowing.

Many cleaning chemicals are hazardous because they are corrosive and can cause skin and eye burns if splashed onto the body. Without proper controls, some may cause dermatitis (dry, sore, flaky skin) or other skin irritations, asthma and breathing problems. It is highly unlikely that any adult would ever think of drinking a cleaning chemical intentionally but it is still common to find food or drink containers being used to store hazardous cleaning substances. Touching the face/eyes/skin after handling a cleaning chemical can cause irritation, inflammation or chemical burns.

Some substances can cause breathing problems if oversprayed, used without adequate ventilation or sprayed onto hot surfaces, for example oven cleaner. There can also be adverse chemical reactions when substances are mixed, for example cleaning products containing bleach mixed with acidic toilet cleaners or ammonia will give off harmful gases. Other risks arise from accidental splashes to the skin and eyes while cleaning chemicals are being poured from one container into another or from spillages while being carried in open containers. There may also be manual handling risks if the containers are heavy or bulky.

For example, an employee poured bleach into an empty spray bottle. A reaction occurred with unknown remains in the bottle, causing the bleach to spurt out of the bottle into the eyes of another employee.

Train staff on use and handling of cleaning chemicals, including instructions not to mix different chemicals and ensure that all containers and spray bottles are clearly labelled with their contents. Provide information on firstaid procedures and what to do in the event of accidental spillages. Provide protective gloves for use when handling.

Another example, an employee was working near the grill, which was being cleaned by the sous chef using caustic oven cleaner. Later that night, she became wheezy and suffered an asthma attack. The following day she consulted her GP suffering from a blister at the back of her throat and burns to her nasal passage. Investigation of this accident revealed that the oven cleaner had been sprayed onto a hot surface, against supplier's recommendations that it should only be used on warm surfaces. The high temperature caused the oven cleaner to boil, producing a harmful vapour (sodium hydroxide) that had drifted. Enquiries also revealed that training had not been given to employees and that the sous chef did not use any personal protective equipment while cleaning.

Train staff on the use and handling of cleaning chemicals, including instruction that hot surfaces should be allowed to cool sufficiently before applying oven cleaner. This would prevent producing harmful fumes. There should be adequate ventilation while the cleaning is underway. Personal protective clothing should be provided when using the substance, eg appropriate gloves, face visor, fume mask, apron, as per manufacturer's recommendations.

Legal Requirements

Legal requirements applying to the use of cleaning chemicals include the Health and Safety at Work etc Act 1974 and, more specifically, the Control of Substances Hazardous to Health Regulations 2002 (COSHH). These require employers to:

— assess the risks that arise from the use of hazardous substances. This will include any arrangements to deal with accidents, incidents or emergencies, such as those resulting from serious spillages. The assessment must also include the health and safety risks arising from storage, handling or disposal of any of the substances;

— prevent, or if this is not reasonably practicable, control the exposure to such substances;

— provide staff with information, instruction and

— training on the risks and the steps and precautions the employer has taken to control these risks, for example provision of appropriate rubber gloves or appropriate eye protection.

Risk assessment of employers

— *Step1*: List all the hazardous chemicals used.

— *Step 2*: Consider whether there is a need to use each substance in the first place. Stop using those that are not required.

— *Step 3*: For each of those substances remaining and for any new cleaning chemicals you later consider, ask your supplier if this is the safest product available or is there a safer alternative, which you should use if it is available. Ask your supplier if you can purchase diluted products in smaller containers that will be easier to use.

— *Step 4*: For all chemicals used, record a description of their use, eg oven cleaner, and a description of the type of hazard they represent, eg irritant/corrosive/toxic etc. It will include instructions on first-aid measures and advice on what to do in case of accidental spillages. If you do not have this information ask your supplier to provide it. Manufacturers and suppliers of hazardous substances are required by law to provide safety information on their products.

— *Step 5*: Consider where and how the chemicals are used or handled. Avoid pouring from and using bulk containers, as these can be heavy and hard to hold. Minimise handling, eg by use of appropriate syphons, pumps etc, use smaller containers, and avoid carrying open containers, especially if floors are wet or slippery.

— *Step 6*: Try to keep chemicals in their original containers and, if decanting, ensure that containers are clearly marked and labelled with the manufacturer's instructions for use. The label should clearly identify the hazards of the substance. This will help to prevent any confusion regarding the contents.

— *Step 7*: Consider the safe storage arrangements—away from heat, sunlight, foodstuffs and members of public, especially children. Containers should all have lids and be clearly labelled. Cleaning and disinfecting chemicals should be securely stored. Always check manufacturers' storage instructions, as some products may need to be stored separately from others.

— *Step 8*: Ensure all your employees are informed, trained, and supervised in the use of cleaning chemicals. It will not be enough just to issue safety data sheets; you must ensure that your employees understand the hazards and the measures needed to control any risks.

— *Step 9*: Take into consideration any of your staff who do not have English as a first language. You must ensure that they clearly understand. Posters or graphics can help as reminders on carrying out the job safely. Employees and their safety representatives should be consulted about health and safety issues including the use of cleaning chemicals. They may have experienced problems or come up with solutions that you may not have considered.

— *Step 10*: Monitor and review employees' use of cleaning chemicals. Supervisors should observe that they are being used and stored correctly. Ensure new employees are trained.

— *Step 11*: Make sure appropriate protective clothing is available when using the cleaning chemical. This could include eye protection, various types of gloves, facemasks and visors etc. Latex gloves are known to cause reactions and should be avoided. Employees must be trained when and how to use and replace such protection.

— *Step 12*: Check first-aid arrangements. Staff should be trained in first-aid actions to take in the event of accidental contact with skin or eyes, and appropriate first-aid provision should be available, eg eyewash bottles. Safety data sheets should be kept in a place known to staff in the event that they need to be referred to in case of spillage or an accident.

Guidance to employees

— Always follow carefully any instructions and training information given in the use of cleaning chemicals.

— Remember that your safety representative and you as an employee are entitled to be consulted by your employer about health and safety issues including the use of cleaning chemicals.

— When handling substances, especially concentrates (if unavoidable), always wear the protective clothing provided, eg rubber gloves. If there is any danger of splashing, wear eye protection suitable for splash risks, eg goggles or visors, and ensure an eyewash bottle is available. If cleaning at eye level or above, wear eye protection.

— Check that rubber gloves are free from holes, tears or thin patches. If any of these faults are present ask for replacements immediately. Tell your employer if you experience any irritation or allergy from gloves you have used.

— Never mix cleaning chemicals.

— When diluting always add the concentrated liquid to water, not the water to the concentrate.

— If cleaning chemicals are accidentally splashed onto your skin or eyes, always wash away with plenty of water. Seek medical advice if irritation persists and tell your employer.

— Avoid lifting and pouring from heavy or awkward bulk containers, minimise handling by use of syphons, pumps etc.

— If you are dispensing powders, always use a scoop; never use your hand.

— Never transfer cleaning chemicals into food or drink containers where they can easily be mistaken for foodstuffs. Ensure spray bottles are other containers are clearly marked with their contents.

— If aerosols are used for cleaning, never spray onto hot surfaces as this can produce harmful vapours. Never place aerosols on hot surfaces.

— Only use cleaning chemicals in well-ventilated areas. Sometimes an open window will be enough, but proper extract ventilation should be installed if fumes are a risk. A suitable fume mask and goggles may also be required depending on manufacturer's instructions.

— Always clean up any spills on floors or work surfaces immediately.

— Always store chemicals as manufacturers advise, for example away from heat, sunlight, foodstuffs and members of the public, especially children.

— Ensure chemicals are disposed of properly, as instructed by your employer following the information given in the safety data sheet.

— Let your supervisor or manager know immediately if you experience any adverse reactions to substances, for example headaches, nausea, skin complaints.

11

Protecting Hotels Against Legal Attacks

Laws are commonly used to explain and to defend their own actions and the actions of others. All law is dynamic, which is contrary to popular opinion that it is concrete and unchanging. Not only does the law move, but such movement is caused by and reflective of the evolution of the society it supports and attempts to influence. It is one's individual decision, as a private citizen, how little or how much of the law with which to become familiar. As a hotelier, however, it is imperative that he becomes familiar with that portion of the law which so deeply and severely affects our industry. Lodging law, like all law, is a living breathing entity which is constantly changing. To ignore it and those changes is to put oneself as a hotelier, in peril.

The laws by which the lodging industry is governed, came from old English common law—that system of legal thought which forms the basis for the laws which exist today in most states. While old basic common law has evolved greatly over the years by judicial precedent, and many exceptions apply, it cannot be overemphasised that protection of the guest is an absolute requirement.

A basic explanation of the law is in order, as it affects us as hoteliers. This is not to say that hoteliers are not governed or influenced by the criminal codes—on the contrary just as every citizen is held to those guidelines and restraints, so also are hoteliers. However, in your day-to-day conduct of lodging business, the civil aspects of the law are the ones with which you most often will come into contact. To state again for emphasis, the most vital civil law lesson which must be learned and practised by lodging professionals is that protection of the guest is an absolute requirement.

Legal Attacks against Hotels

The former California Governor Gray Davis signed into law Senate Bill 796, aka the Bounty Hunter Law. It creates a new "private right of action" so that California employees can sue their employers for most violations of the California Labor Code. Prevailing plaintiffs may recover lost wages plus significant civil penalties and attorneys' fees. Although Governor Schwarzenegger recently signed modest reforms to the law, the most significant provisions of the legislation remain intact and continue to adversely impact employers.

Plaintiffs' attorneys have sprung into action, loaded their weapons and filed a variety of these Bounty Hunter lawsuits against employers based on workplace posting violations, unlawful pre-employment inquiries in employment applications, failure to provide rest breaks and meal periods, unlawful pay practices and wage deductions and almost invariably, a claim for violations of California Unfair Competition Laws.

In June 2004, California hospitality employers Wolfgang Puck Casual Dining, Crystal Park, Hollywood Park and Bell Gardens Bicycle Club casinos, among numerous others, were targeted in Bounty Hunter class action lawsuits. Common allegations against the casinos include the casinos' requiring card dealers to buy casino chips or post a bond payment in order to take possession of a bank to perform their job duties. Dealers purportedly were required to take responsibility for any loss to the bank at the end of their work shift. Also, the casinos allegedly required dealers to make a payment to the casino out of any earned tips at the end of every half-hour work rotation, regardless if they received any tips during the work rotations.

Allegations against Wolfgang Puck Casual Dining include the company's failure to provide non-exempt employees with rest and meal periods, failure to provide additional compensation for working through rest and meal periods, failure to provide additional compensation for split shifts, and failure to pay such wages upon termination of employment. The plaintiffs also allege that the company failed to maintain required time records, failed to provide employees with appropriate wage statements and unlawfully required employees to purchase uniforms.

Steps for Reducing the Risk

Understand wage and hour obligations. Regularly review with human resources personnel their current obligations. Consult labor and employment counsel to confirm proper interpretation of current obligations.

Classify employees properly. Multi-state employers should know that the federal wage and hour exemptions have been changed, effective as of August 2004. The minimum salary requirement for exempt status jumped from $250 to $455 per week, resulting in fewer employees being properly classified as exempt. Marketing and inside sales persons are often misclassified as exempt employees because their job duties usually do not meet the requirements. Outside salespersons are only exempt if they spend at least 50% of their time away from the employer's business location selling services or products.

Maintain time records. To guard against meritless claims and minimise exposure to valid claims, employers must maintain adequate and accurate time records, maintain express policies governing time records, and provide training to ensure compliance.

Review wage and hour policies. Ensure that your written policies fully comply with applicable law. This is currently an explosive area for dangerous class action lawsuits.

Audit wage and hour practices. If your company already has policies, they must be properly implemented. Review the company's written policies and, through direct consultation with employees at different levels, look for disparities between company policy and practice.

Issue new or revised written policies as necessary. If written policies or practices do not comport with applicable wage and hour laws, you should remedy deficiencies immediately. Start right away with new written policies complying with applicable law and affirming the company's ongoing commitment to such compliance.

Training supervisors and managers. When new or corrected policies or procedures are issued, supervisory employees must understand their proper implementation.

Training is critical. Although competent human resources professionals can implement these recommendations, counsel should review new or current policies and procedures for deficiencies and ambiguities that invite wage and hour attacks by Bounty Hunters.

Policies To Avoid Lawsuits from Disabled Hotel Guests

Inappropriate action can be a violation of the Americans With Disabilities Act (ADA) and additional state laws in California and many other states. The ADA applies in all 50 states, and to all types of properties open to the public, whether hotels, restaurants, sports facilities, stadiums, wineries, retail stores, apartment houses or senior living facilities. In fact, the problem is serious enough that it received attention in May 2004 from the influential 9th Circuit Court of Appeal.

The liability-creating issue relates to accommodating disabled guests with service animals. This is entirely independent from the question of whether or not your hotel or restaurant has a "no pet" or "pet friendly" policy. According to the law, service animals are not pets. Service animals are specifically trained to protect, aid, alert and provide their owners with mobility and independence. Health codes that prohibit animals in restaurants, for example, do not apply to service animals.

California law recognizes "service canines," such as sight or guide dogs, signal dogs and seizure alert dogs, but under the ADA, the definition or service animals includes any type of animal individually trained by the disabled person or someone else, to provide assistance. No discrimination against disabled guests with service animals. Under the ADA, hotels and all other public accommodations are required to treat disabled guests with service animals like all other guests; namely, they are to be provided the same services and access to all areas of the property where other guests are generally allowed.

While most service animals are trained guide dogs, the ADA applies to any individually trained animal. Service monkeys or cats have been encountered. The potential for abuse is obvious, but how far can you probe?

Guests with service animals should be welcomed and provided access to all areas where guests are normally allowed, such as pool areas, laundries, business centers, restaurants, lobbies, etc. If a guest says that he or she is disabled and the animal is a service animal, that should be the end of it. Check the guest in without further inquiry on the subject. Otherwise, you are just asking for a letter from an ADA activist enforcement group.

If other guests complain of the mere presence of the service animal, staff should explain the law requires hotels to let disabled guests have service animals. If the service animal becomes unreasonably disruptive or threatening, the owner is responsible for controlling the animal. However, most service animals are particularly trained to be around people and are not dangerous and they are quite tidy. If the service animal becomes dangerous or disruptive, they can be removed, but the disabled guest should be welcome to stay without the animal.

Hotel operators are not required to provide special services like food, water, doggy bags, leashes, etc. Staff is not required to clean a service animal's mess, but if staff cleans the rooms generally and put guest items away, they should do the same with the animal's accoutrements. Hotels cannot impose a separate charge or cleaning deposit for service animals, even if it generally charges for pets. However, like any other guest, the disabled person is responsible for cleaning up after the animal, protecting the public from vicious animals, and paying to repair any damage to the property. The animal's owner is responsible for supervising and caring for it.

With these overriding principles, the bottom line is, if a person says she or he is disabled and that the animal is a service animal, staff should accept the statements as true and permit the guest and the animal to stay. Staff can specifically ask the potential guest what kind of assistance the animal provides, but that's all. Staff can neither ask the individual to prove their disability nor inquire about the nature of the disability. Staff cannot demand any certification or proof that the animal is a "service animal."

In May, 2004, the 9th Circuit handed down a decision regarding service animals. In Lentini v. California Center for the Arts, the Center tried to bar a disabled patron and a yapping dog (which yapped to warn the owner of people in close proximity) from attending a concert performance because the dog was allegedly previously disruptive. When plaintiff and her service animal refused to leave the Center, she was threatened with arrest. The Court observed that dogs bark, even at concerts. The Center had to modify its policies to allow the disabled patron to attend performances with a service animal that may have made disruptive noises at past performances if such behavior would have been acceptable if engaged in by humans (warning, not barking!).

The court said the noise the animal makes is for a valid reason (i.e., to warn the owner) and humans would be permitted to voice the same warning. The Center had to accommodate the dog. The court held Center staff failed to consider the reasons why a service animal would make noise and without the modifications to the policy, individuals like the plaintiff, would be excluded from future performances. Humans certainly can scream out "Fire" if there is one. So too can a service animal alert its owner. The Center unsuccessfully argued the admission of the service animal would fundamentally alter the nature of the services by disrupting the performances. However, the court found the Center failed to prove the dog's yipping would necessarily be disruptive. Thus, the court recognised under certain circumstances where the animal was disruptive, unrelated to it's service function, it could be removed or excluded.

There were no complaints from patrons. The Center's manager and another employee lied about the incident. Bad facts! The Center and its two employees were ordered to pay monetary damages to the plaintiff. The court went on to say intentional discriminatory conduct was not required to recover the $4,000 minimum statutory damages under the Unruh Civil Rights Act. The court awarded damages for the actual evening plaintiff was excluded and for the next 6 performances she proved she would have attended but for defendants' policies and practices.

Development of Pet Policies

Most hotels have developed "Pet Policies," either prohibiting pets or imposing reasonable restrictions such as the type and number of pets, confining pets to certain areas, leash requirements, requiring owners to clean up after their pets, to furnish their own pet services, impose pet fees and cleaning deposits and removal of noisy or disruptive pets. Such policies are perfectly appropriate for "Pets." Service animals are not pets—so many policies that apply to pets are simply illegal if applied to service animals. A carefully drawn policy for pets and service animals can help avoid embarrassing encounters and expensive litigation.

Ways to Protect Hotels from Legal Attacks

How can you dramatically reduce legal attacks while building a wall of defense around your company? Follow these ten simple steps and you will be on your way to protecting your company by building a fortress of defense.

1. Investigate and take action on all reports of harassment and discrimination. All managers and directors must report to the human resources director or other personnel any and all incidences or claims made by employees in connection with sexual

harassment or any other type of harassment or discrimination. If managers do not report the incident or claim and an investigation does not occur, the company is at risk. Every employee should undergo annual anti-harassment and anti-discrimination training. The company's policy of prohibiting harassment and discrimination of any kind should be clear, in writing, and effectively communicated to every employee. Newly hired employees, as well as seasoned veterans, need this training. During any investigation, if new incidences are discovered, those incidences should also be thoroughly investigated. A report, which includes written statements of witnesses and the resolution of the claims, needs to be well documented and placed in the appropriate personnel file.

2. Make sure all agreements with vendors and suppliers are in writing and their insurance has not expired. The financial officer of each hotel or restaurant should undertake a careful review of all agreements. Be particularly mindful of indemnification clauses (in which one person agrees to protect another person from claims by third parties), waivers and releases, automatic renewals of the term of the agreement and assignment clauses that prohibit the hotel or restaurant from transferring the agreement to a new purchaser or new operator. Make sure all vendor and supplier agreements allow for the hotel or restaurant to cancel for any reason or no reason on thirty-(30) day's written notice. Obtain current certificates of insurance from every vendor and supplier and ask for updated certificates periodically. Make certain that the insurance certificate lists the hotel or restaurant operating or managing company, as well as the owner of the establishment, as additional insured parties on the policy.

3. Keep accurate maintenance logs on all equipment. Many cases have been settled or lost in court due to the failure of the property owner to maintain accurate maintenance logs on equipment owned or serviced by a hotel. This includes the monthly, quarterly or annual maintenance checks on elevators, bicycles, fitness equipment, pool equipment, etc. It is important to maintain clear and accurate records to show a judge, jury or opposing lawyer the diligence that went in to ensuring the property was safe. Among other things, the records should reflect the times and dates of inspection, any and all repairs made and the name(s) of the qualified employee(s) responsible for maintaining the records. Accidents happen, of course, but an accurate maintenance log will go a long way in reducing your liability.
4. Follow all rules for proper notification to guests of in-room telephone charges. Due to the popularity of cell phones and PDAs, hotel guestroom telephone usage has declined. However, many hoteliers may not be aware that there are federal and state laws stating what must be clearly communicated to your guests prior to them making telephone calls from guestrooms. Written notice of all fees and charges must be given to the callers in the guestrooms as directed by the statutes, and should be featured in a prominent location. The in-room guest directory should include the following information and applicable charges: local calls, directory assistance, alternate carrier access (for other long distance carriers than the one the hotel does business with), toll free calls, international calls and long distance calls.
5. Don't send unsolicited faxes to customers without their written permission. The 1991 Federal Telephone Consumer Protection Act prohibits the sending of unsolicited fax advertisements in all states. Specifically,

business owners are not allowed to send unsolicited faxes that advertise the commercial availability or quality of property, goods or services to customers without first obtaining their permission. The recipient of such faxes can successfully sue the sender and collect $500 per fax. Plus, if they can prove you willfully violated the law, they could recover $1500 per violation. Although some companies are challenging this law based on First Amendment issues, until the law is changed, compliance will eliminate these claims.

6. Have all employees who pour, serve or sell alcohol beverages, and all managers, attend an alcohol awareness programme. Not only is it important for this training to occur, your legal adviser (and most likely, your insurance carrier) will insist that your employees learn the legal basics of pouring, serving and selling alcohol beverages to your patrons and guests. Most states have "dram shop laws" that require establishments to adhere to alcohol safety and awareness standards. If someone leaves your establishment and is personally injured or injures another person or property, the patron's lawyer will look to the establishment to see if alcohol was consumed on the premises. Be smart and implement preventative measures now.
7. Have a written email policy prohibiting jokes, off-color remarks, and other potentially offensive activities. As part of their lawsuits against companies, plaintiffs are requesting that defendant companies produce all email transmissions in order to collection incriminating information about the company and its employees. These messages, although may appear to be deleted by each user, are not gone forever. They actually are maintained on back-up tapes that carry this information forever (at least a very long time until

they are erased by an IT professional). Remind employees that although email messages appear to be a quick and casual way of communicating, it can be hazardous to your company's bottom line. Advise them not to put anything in an email message that they would not want to see as a headline in your daily newspaper. Every company's written email policy should require all employees to avoid creating, viewing or forwarding offensive or inappropriate emails or Internet postings related to a person's race, color, national origin, religion, sex, sexual orientation, age, disability or veteran status. Also, they should avoid creating, viewing or forwarding jokes, cartoon, games or chain letters. The email policy should also provide for immediate disciplinary action or termination of employment, if necessary, for violations.

8. Be aware of scams. There are numerous scams ongoing for many years that managers need to be aware of and need to educate all employees. For example, con artists are targeting companies with the Nigerian letter scam. This scam begins with a letter or message that is mailed, faxed or emailed informing a business that there is a certain surplus of funds that exist and by providing your business bank account information to hold these funds for a short time, the business will receive a portion of these funds. This is an attempt to empty your company's bank account. Also, be aware that certain companies may be marketing a hotel directory that is not pre-approved or in line with your company's marketing strategies. An unsuspecting employee may obligate your company by agreeing to a long-term commitment to have your property listed in the directory.

9. Inform your guests about laptop computer theft. In too many cases, laptop computers are left in hotel meeting rooms and are easy targets for thieves. To

anticipate your guest's needs, provide a safe to store laptop computers when not in use or when the group is taking a break from their meeting. Provide computer-cabling locks to assist your guests in securing their laptops. Lock or control entry to meeting rooms when not in use. While not a preventative measure, hoteliers can also post a warning in the area so that the hotel is not responsible for stolen or damaged property. Prior to posting the sign, review your state's limitation of liability statute to determine your liability in such cases.

10. Don't release guest information to anyone other than the guest. Releasing guest information to the wrong person can result in a claim being filed against your property. Guests have a certain expectation of privacy that needs to be acknowledged and recognised by all employees. A written policy needs to be established whereby (i) the registered guest makes the request in person and either the guest is recognised by the employee or provides sufficient identification or (ii) the guest submits a signed, written request and the hotel or motel is able to verify that the signature belongs to the registered guest. Certain exceptions to the policy would include those circumstances when the hotel or motel is compelled by law to produce the guest information (a court order or subpoena, for example) or when a crime has been committed against the hotel or motel.

12

Crisis Management

We live in ever-changing times, where consumers are increasingly aware, lawyers are ever more litigious and the media increasingly willing to expose any weakness in a hospitality organisation or tourist destination. A company or region in the midst of a crisis cannot completely control these factors, as events in Asia Pacific have demonstrated loud and clear over the past 12 months. However, sufficient preparation and effective management can take the edge off the above factors.

Companies and destinations are now realising that they not only have a moral obligation, but also may need to take a legal stance to be prepared to cope with incidents that involve their clients. Planning, though critical, is not the only component. Training, conducting drills, testing procedures and providing additional external resources are other important functions. By doing the above, organisations can go a long way to emerging from such incidents with their reputations and/or corporate image intact.

The lessons learned in Bali are manifold and must be now used to prepare other destinations, as well as all their stakeholders—including hotels—for future crises. In essence, the following "components" are required in order to handle any crisis situation effectively:

— Leadership (crisis coordination);
— Adequate emergency response (ambulance/paramedics/medical support);
— Victim identification;
— Media relations;
— Family assistance;
— Information dissemination;
— Internal and external communications.

An effective emergency response and good family assistance will reduce the frustrations that many people experience when caught up in the aftermath of a major incident. Besides going a long way to ensuring effective crisis management, it is also a humane, caring and compassionate way to respond. Few crises will seem as dramatic as New York or Bali—unless it is your own. When your crisis occurs, the hardest part of dealing with it can involve answering the public call for information—as personified by a TV correspondent or newspaper reporter who shows up on your doorstep or on your telephone line to get the story.

While the existence of some of the above components may be based on the assumption of the pre-existence of a structured and experienced emergency services (police, fire and ambulance), this would be an unrealistic expectation, in many situations. However, there are still some basic steps that governments/regions can look at in order to enhance their level of preparedness. This involves the triad of:

— Planning (developing written plans);
— Training (selecting and training the initial crisis responders); and
— Regular rehearsals (conducting "major incident" exercises).

Local governments—or, even better, regional organisation like ASEANTA and/or PATA—could take the lead in this, and enhance their image, by

— Creating awareness amongst the industry;

— Organising training sessions for all stakeholders; and

— Communicating their efforts to the consumer.

The key to success is intensive training, although indepth consultations towards establishing the exact needs of the participants is needed to tailor the final curricula to local, regional and inter-regional training activities. The focus of the training sessions must be on senior and intermediate levels of management, with the aim that, by the end of the course, all those attending will be knowledgeable about the following :

1. Before the Crisis
   - What constitutes a real crisis;
   - Why crisis management is necessary;
   - Assessing potential crisis issues;
   - Crisis-management team responsibilities;
   - Setting up the emergency communication system; and
   - Major elements of crisis management planning.
2. During and after the Crisis
   - Structuring the media centre;
   - Designating spokespersons;
   - Preparing "message points";
   - Interview techniques and guidelines;
   - Controlling the story; and
   - Starting the "back-to-normal" plans.

In almost every instance of successful response to a crisis, management and response activities consisting of sound operating execution, coupled with superior communications, predominate. Operational response is essential—it's the one that saves lives, property and other assets. The ability to communicate is no less important—it's the one that saves the business. The simple fact is: perception is reality, and public perception of your company's reaction to a crisis is as important as your operating response.

There are no clear boundaries with any crisis. There is rarely a single moment when one can say an incident or issue has transformed into a crisis. Crisis-management experts recommend adopting a low threshold when defining a crisis, erring on the side of caution and assuming that a small episode can escalate into a crisis at warp speed. The repercussions and impact of crises in tourism is manifested across a series of stakeholders. To avert mismanagement of crises and its consequences, organisations and destinations need to enhance their capacity to understand and respond to crisis situations.

Crisis Communication Programme

If no crisis communications programme is in place, there is no better time to create and implement one. Crisis preparedness is essential for protecting a property or brand's image and safeguarding its reputation as a safe and welcoming travel destination. Although terrorist incidents have dominated the recent news, there are many kinds of crisis that can impact a property's ability to service guests and conduct or build business. These include:

- Fire
- Labour strikes or unrest
- Kidnapping or hostage-taking
- Assault or other crimes committed on, or by, hotel personnel or line staff

— Natural disasters such as hurricanes, earthquakes or floods

Importance of a Plan

Crisis management is a field endeavor unto itself, and the surest way to stay prepared is to work with a specialist to create a programme that meets your needs. Short of that, start by creating a communications plan that enables your team to respond in a rational, systematic and effective way should a crisis situation arise. Here are some elements that such a plan should include:

A clear chain of command among responsible management and staff: In the event of a crisis, it should be clear who is designated to investigate and gather the facts, who will report to whom, and who will serve as the property's liaison to guests, employees and the media. Participants in this group may include the property's general manager, marketing personnel, human resources and department heads.

Lists of critical phone numbers, fax and e-mail contact information: Every member of the group should be able to reach and talk to any other member at a moment's notice, including in the event of a power outage. Relevant members of the group should also have direct contact information for important off-property individuals who may become important players, such as property owners, police and fire authorities, federal authorities, lawyers and key vendors.

Designation of a spokesperson to handle media inquiries—and media relations training: Hotels are diffuse operations, with dozens, hundreds or even thousands of individuals working on property at any given time. Every hotel or corporate brand management team should have one or two individuals who are solely responsible for speaking to the media on the property's behalf at a time of crisis. The most important point is making sure that the property speaks to the public with a single voice—and that the voice is one of calm, reason and reassurance. The best way of assuring reasoned, effective communication with the media is to provide training for your spokespeople from professionals who perform "media relations" for a living.

Understanding your audiences: While communicating with the media is important—and can be the "make or break" factor in managing a crisis successfully –, there are many other critical actors with whom you will want to communicate effectively at a time of crisis. These may include current and future guests, line staff and management personnel, stockholders or shareholders, local public officials and authorities, key vendors and families/ associates of victims of a crisis. In planning to confront a potential crisis in the future, make lists of these key audiences now, and update them regularly.

Understanding the Media

PR professionals earn their livelihood working with the media. Responding effectively in a crisis situation can be the most challenging task of all. Some basic principles are:

Know your local media contacts personally: A crisis situation is no time to start winning friends and influencing people. By establishing good relationships with key media in your community—a sound and valuable practice for any hotel at any time –, you create an environment of trust and open communication should a crisis arise. This is key for assuring that the right facts are communicated to the public via the media, quickly, efficiently and comprehensively.

Let your lawyer, designated crisis team leader and/or spokesperson do the talking: Again, the principle is to speak with one voice—and make that voice the right one. Depending on the situation, it may be appropriate to prepare written statements to guide spokespersons and to issue written statements to the press. Such statements should be drafted and carefully reviewed with legal, financial and other experts.

Cooperate with the media, as with all investigating authorities—and never say "no comment": The media has a job to do, and that job is reporting the facts and the news to the public. In a crisis situation, returning media calls promptly and being forthcoming will let reporters know that you want to help them do their job—and the likely result of that is balanced, fair coverage. In a crisis situation, designated spokespersons with a clear understanding of the facts and the important messages to be conveyed should share information with reporters in a prudent but timely way, and should keep clear and concise records of what they say.

If the facts of the situation are not clear, journalists should be assured that all efforts are being made to get all the facts on table, and should be kept updated regularly. Saying "no comment" conveys a sense of arrogance or ignorance and prevents you from framing your story and getting the facts out as fully as possible. In contacts with the media, that phrase should be avoided at all costs.

Emergency Management

Managing emergencies and providing safety and security to guests, customers, employees, owners, and the property itself, requires informed and thorough planning and organisation across the board, with the active involvement of all departments and employees. This responsibility cannot be relegated to only a few people in the organisation. And these subjects cannot be considered as a "separate" field, but become an integral part of all operational functions. A Safety and Security Committee must be selected (appointed or elected by the management team), based on the ability of its members to plan, communicate, train, coordinate, delegate, implement, supervise, and control the many aspects related to the prevention and management of safety, security and emergency situations pertinent to the organisation.

This committee must be an active and dynamic force representing various operational departments (or divisions). Appointment to the committee should be based on knowhow, experience, and the ability to coordinate, implement and train, rather than rank. Rank-and-file and supervisory levels often make part of such committees. The chairperson (and vice-chair) of the committee establish direct contact with national (federal) and local government authorities, obtain updated regulations and information, and obtain assistance and guidance from these authorities who are always glad to provide it.

For example, they can invite the fire department to speak to different departments about fire hazards and prevention, or invite the police department to provide training and guidance on matters of security. Government authorities gladly give training material such as videos, posters, and print material for distribution. A regular schedule is set for training by outsiders and "in house" continuous training for all departments. Sporadic spot checks and drills are conducted.

The committee plans ahead for emergencies, such as fire outbreaks or other manmade or natural disasters, makes sure specific duties are assigned, such as immediate reporting to higher management, the security officer in charge, local authorities (such as the fire brigade). Supervisors and employees receive clear instructions and training on how to alert and rescue customers, guests, and visitors, including body count after evacuation, as well as how to alert other departments and colleagues. The key concern in all cases of disaster is to avoid panic.

Sometimes more lives are lost due to panic than due to the emergency itself. A fail-proof communications network is set up, decided upon, different departments and individuals are assigned roles with clearly written explanations of, and discussions on, duties to perform in such events. People are taught to constantly keep aware of risks and hazards, and are trained on how to proceed, including providing feedback to the committee who can then take corrective measures.

The most important point to remember when organising for emergency handling, safety and security, is that this is not the work of a few but an overall organisational effort. Though basic principles are the same, actual planning and organisation differ from one organisation to the other, depending upon its setup, nature, type of clientele, type of service, staffing, management and employee profiles.

Disaster Management

Since the specter of terrorist activity has risen in our collective consciousness—and the images of hurricanes Charley and Frances have swept across out television screens—hotel owners and operators worldwide are blowing the dust off of their disaster plans. Whether the cause is terrorists or hurricane, fire, flood, earthquake, or other disaster, the smart money knows that the best time to deal with an emergency is before it happens.

Maintain safe conditions. Keeping your premises safe can save lives. It can also help in defending against allegations of negligence should a disaster occur. Consider the lesson of the hotel that let dust and linen accumulate in linen chutes: when the accumulation caused an otherwise containable fire to spread and cause substantial damage, they were held liable. Test he alarm and emergency communications systems regularly. During an emergency, you must be able to alert your guests, deploy personnel, and summon emergency services quickly.

Keep your emergency plan current. The evacuation guides on the back of hotel room doors do not constitute an "emergency plan." Your plan should ensure that guests receive adequate warning of an emergency and provide for their effective evacuation. Your plan should provide for ongoing education to employees and for conducting periodic drills to ensure compliance with the plan. Employee training should reflect geographic realities: danger comes in the form of hurricanes in the Caribbean and Southeast, tsunamis in the Pacific Rim, tornados in the Midwest, and earthquakes in California.

Warn guests of the emergency. You have a duty to warn guests of an emergency: do not delay! Liability check: Hotels can be held liable for a failure to warn guests of an emergency or for an unduly delayed warning. You may not have to physically accompany guests out of the hotel, but you can be held liable if blocked exists or inadequate lighting in halls and stairwells impedes evacuation. Call for medical assistance. Hotels have a legal obligation to call for medical assistance when a guest is seriously ill or suffers serious injury.

If your hotel is safe, don't raise the rates. If your hotel survives a disaster and other hotels in the vicinity do not survive, the market value of your safe hotel rooms will skyrocket. However, think twice before raising your rates. In Florida, Attorney General Charlie Crist has filed at least two civil complaints against hotels for alleged price gouging an deceptive and unfair trade practices of consumers seeking shelter from Hurricane Charley.

13

Employees' Role in Hotel Protection

The owners and the managers of an operation are legally liable for any accidents, illness and death caused by negligence with regard to Safety and Security, vis-a-vis the courts and vis-a-vis the company's insurers. Policies and procedures must be complete, with clearly written instructions. Communications to both in-house personnel and to guests must also be "wholesome", effective and clear. Training strategies and activities must be clearly written, with scheduled planned and historic records. This applies also to repairs and maintenance schedules, drills, and committee meetings. The above is not written based on theory but on actual successful experience in organising the best safety and security handling in the service industry.

Liability of Employees

Liability of Innkeeper

As a general rule an innkeeper cannot deny lodging to a guest on the basis of age. Since many high school seniors are 18 years old, they are protected by many state laws against unfair discrimination. An innkeeper must then have reasonable cause for rejecting a request for lodging. In many states, 18 year olds may file unfair discrimination lawsuits and seek financial damages. 18 year olds are, however, under the legal drinking age in most states. This allows innkeepers to restrict room rental if alcohol is present. This does not mean that an innkeeper cannot establish preconditions and rules for accepting a minor as a guest.

Certainly, the innkeeper is well-advised to inform a minor that any behaviour that disturbs other guests, or involves drinking or drugs will lead to eviction. The minor should be informed that only registered guests are allowed in the room. Requiring prepayment is always advisable with notice to the minor guest that eviction will not result in a refund. Innkeepers may wish to consider copying identification or having the minor sign an acknowledgement that he or she has read house rules. Any reasonable grounds that would permit an innkeeper to reject a request for lodging or evict an adult will generally be applicable to minors. Innkeepers have the right to evict minors who violate house rules or commit illegal acts such as consumption of alcoholic beverages while under age 21.

However, the innkeeper must exercise reasonable care in avoiding physical force. An innkeeper should not jeopardize the safety of a minor guest by eviction in a high crime area or where minor may encounter a hazardous situation. The innkeeper should consider contacting the police for assistance or even calling the minor's parents. The enactment of the following procedures by hotel personnel should help make this prom and graduation season a more enjoyable one for your hotel.

— Inform guests that only registered guests are allowed in the room

— Guests must fully complete a registration form.

— Require prepayment with a deposit. Notify guests that eviction will not result in a refund.

— Guests must conform with house rules. Any behaviour that disturbs other guests, or involves drinking or drugs will require hotel to contact the police and assist in eviction.

— Ask guests for picture identification and keep a copy for your records.

Talk to schools in your area and find out when the proms and dances are scheduled so that you will be prepared. Inform all minors making reservations of the preconditions in advance and then have them sign the attached form before checking in. In addition, we advise contacting local authorities to get up to speed on local laws governing commerce with minors. Most importantly, make sure hotel personnel are trained on your hotel's policies for renting to minors.

Liability of Employees

Lay-offs often beget litigation as former employees sue their former employers in a scramble to maximise cash and get retribution. In this fray, hospitality employers need to understand the complex web of state and federal laws that govern their liability or face big losses that offset sought-after savings sought from workforce reductions.

Discrimination, harassment and retaliation claims

Employers making lay-offs should expect discrimination, harassment and retaliation claims. Some employees may claim that they are being singled out because of past issues involving harassment or discrimination or because they are being "targeted" for the lay-off or termination based on age, race, national origin, religion, disability, gender or any number of other "protected categories" under the law. Unfortunately, it is not a complete defence for the employer to argue that "business necessity" required the adverse action.

For example, in a claim involving retaliation, the employer will have to demonstrate that it properly dealt with the discrimination or harassment claim originally and that such claim had no causal connection with the decision to lay-off or terminate the individual later. Similarly, in a discrimination claim involving the allegation that certain employees in a protected category are "targeted," the employer will have to demonstrate that there are solid business reasons for choosing one employee or group of employees over others. To minimise claims of this nature, employers should have enforceable arbitration programmes in place that comply with recent Supreme Court guidelines for enforceability.

Also, employers should analyse all lay-off or reorganisation decisions with counsel to ensure that no workers in protected categories — such as individuals over 40—are disproportionately affected by the adverse employment action. Personnel files should be reviewed to flag possible issues involving past claims of harassment or discrimination that could lead to retaliation claims. Employment policies and procedures should be reviewed and updated to ensure that the adverse employment action is in compliance with existing policies and procedures. In addition, all actions which result in lay-offs or job reductions should be appropriately documented and reviewed by counsel.

Relations between employers and management

Hospitality industry employers with unionised work forces have additional contractual and legal obligations which affect the employer's right to eliminate jobs. Most labour agreements contain lay-off clauses which typically obligate the employer to paying severance, benefits and, in some instances, early retirement incentives. Lay-off clauses may also restrict both the elimination of certain jobs and the number of employees that may be laid off. In some instances, they may mandate that the employer follow a specified order in the lay-offs.

In addition to contractual obligations, the National Labour Relations Act imposes a duty on employers to engage in "effects bargaining" with a union whenever there are unionised workforce reductions. During effects bargaining, unions often make additional demands regarding the payout of severance and benefits and the application of seniority with respect to lay-offs. Typically, unions will demand that seniority — not qualifications or competency — be the determining factor in lay-offs. This may not be in the best interest of an employer who wants to maintain the highest level of customer service while streamlining its operations.

Where the employer has cash flow problems, it may be difficult to pay hefty severance packages. Some labour agreements contain "force majeure" or other emergency clauses which employers may invoke, under the right circumstances, to circumvent onerous contractual obligations. Indeed, several air carriers denied furloughed airline workers severance pay and other lay-off benefits when the airlines invoked force majeure clauses immediately after September 11.

Hospitality employers faced with the prospect of reducing a unionised workforce should consider the cost and operational implications triggered by adherence to union demands or contractual obligations. Alternatives, such as loopholes in the collective bargaining agreement or the possible renegotiation, mid-term, of certain contract provisions should be considered.

Payment of wages

Employers are subject to state and federal laws regulating the payment of final wages and other benefits upon an employee's termination, even where there are no WARN Act or union obligations. The general rule is that employees who are discharged or laid off must be paid on the last day of work for all wages earned, including accrued vacation, through the end of their employment. In addition to accrued vacation, employers must pay terminated employees in cash for any accrued time off if set forth in a policy, whether the time-off was accrued under a paid time-off policy or by agreement to receive compensatory time-off in lieu of overtime hours worked.

"Wages" that must be paid upon termination may also include commission and bonus arrangements that were entered into with employees during more economically healthy times. While an employer's failure to pay wages promptly to a terminated employee may result in waiting time penalties, in addition to the monies owed, there are certain circumstances in which employers may be able to forestall or avoid paying other types of compensation, such as commissions or bonuses. For example, depending on how the commission or bonus arrangement was structured with the employee, the employer may have a contractual defence that no commission was owed at all at the time of the employee's termination. Employers should review existing commission and bonus arrangements to determine their applicability to certain business risks and uncertainty.

Once decisions are made with respect to employment terminations, it may be too late to rearrange commission or bonus structures. Before these decisions are made is the time for employers to review commission, bonus plans, vacation and other benefit policies, to redefine them in a manner more employer-sensitive to adverse economic conditions.

Benefits of lay-offs

One often overlooked area of law applicable to employee lay-offs is the employer's obligation to provide the opportunity for continuing health coverage to terminated employees. When an employer provides medical coverage to its employees, and it does so pursuant to the terms of a benefit plan sponsored and administered by the employer, the plan will be subject to regulation under ERISA. Such requirements usually include continuation coverage rights to employees and their dependents under COBRA. On the other hand, if the employer is going out of business or has been acquired by a successor, the COBRA obligation may be eliminated or passed on to a successor employer.

Employers often wonder if lay-off decisions can affect employees who are on a leave of absence. For example, can employers institute job eliminations or reductions that will result in the termination of employees who are out on pregnancy leave, disability leave, workers' compensation leave or family and medical leave? The answer will typically depend on a variety of factors, but most significantly the business reasons for the lay-off and whether the lay-off evenly affects both active employees as well as employees on a leave of absence. To minimise the risk of retaliation claims by employees on a leave of absence whose positions are eliminated, employers must properly document the business reasons supporting the lay-off decisions and consult with labour counsel to consider the risks involved in such decisions.

Pre-employment verification

Employment is a continuum which ranges on and on for any given employee. Pre-employment verification is considered by many experts to be the paramount one available—particularly against crime. Why should this be so? The answer is at the same time rather simple and rather astounding. Consider the entire array of crimes which might befall a guest: armed robbery, room theft, criminal assault, battery, to name only a few. In virtually every case, proximity to the guest-victim is a necessary ingredient. And who has more close proximity than the employee? While this question may seem cold-hearted and disloyal, it is a consideration with which all hoteliers must deal.

Hoteliers must accept the fact that while employees are the most vital of all assets, they also constitute an often unrecognised threat on the protection management matrix. The hotelier must be totally satisfied that the person finally selected for employment is the one most qualified, the one most appropriate, the one most suited, and above all the one most trustworthy. The hotelier, in other words, must do proper, extensive and systematic pre-employment verification.

When our nation was predominantly rural with the majority of the population located in small towns and communities, the task of selecting the best qualified applicant was relatively easy. Today, the prospective employer is faced with a myriad of difficult decisions when the prospect of employing a person must be faced. When properly accomplished, however, these early steps in the employment process allow for an eventual workforce which can be superlative.

Failure, however, to effectively do pre-employment verification can result in untold difficulties ranging from needless lost time and effort to adverse effects on the bottom line, to and including tragic results. The employment process, in its entirety, must conform to all laws and regulations. There are federal, state and local requirements which must be understood and complied with—and different requirements exist in different locations. Hoteliers must become knowledgeable about the laws which affect them in their particular locale. To do otherwise invites great difficulty and possible sanction. And these laws are changing virtually on a daily basis.

Hoteliers must not only know and abide by these laws but keep continually aware of them and their changing status. It is equally critical to note that consideration of the employment process—particularly the pre-employment verification portion—is not something that is normally considered as being part of guest protection and reasonable care. One major part of the protection begins with the property's employment process, particularly pre-employment verification. While this function may be and often is centred in the human resources department, it is indeed a property-wide consideration.

Application Forms

Application forms are as varied in form and design as properties differ one from the other. They are alike, however, in that they often are the first clue that the hiring authority has in determining the qualifications of an applicant. While the form should be designed to elicit sufficient information to assist in the selection process, it should only include only those questions which tire pertinent to the job in question. Subjects to be avoided include inquiries regarding national origins, race, colour, political affiliations, religion, sex, marital status, economic status, and number of children. The components of the application form may vary somewhat but certain basic information is called for on virtually all of them. This includes:

— *Applicant's personal data section*: Full name, current address, telephone number and social security number.

— *Background data section*: Pertinent job-related personal background data which includes both education and experience.

— *References section*: Names of persons who can attest to his abilities, character, education and reliability.

— *Disclaimers section*: Normally in bold and clearly stated fashion immediately above the signature block, the applicant is informed of drug testing policy and policy of the property to engage in background verification including earlier employment criminal background and personal references. It should be stated that the property may use any or all job-related verification techniques which the property manager plans to utilise.

— *Accuracy verification and information release authorisation section*: Typical application forms include statements regarding acknowledgment of the applicant that the information supplied is complete and accurate to the best of his knowledge. Any deliberate falsifications, misrepresentations or omissions may be grounds for not hiring or for subsequent dismissal if hiring has taken place. This is normally followed by a request that the applicant authorise the property to verify all information.

The application form begins with a review of the application form itself.

— *Total form completeness*: Has the applicant completed every required blank and answered every required question? If not, the hotelier may wish to go no further but rather return it to the applicant for completion. For example, many application forms ask the question: "Have you ever been convicted of a felony?" Applicants may choose to ignore this question, often out of fear that disclosing such a history will disqualify them from consideration but fearful also of lying on the application. They decide instead simply to leave that question unanswered.

— *Specific question completeness*: Has the applicant addressed the totality of each question to the satisfaction of the hiring authority? For example, in the space requesting earlier employment job duties an applicant might indicate "supervised staff". This minimum response does not allow an ample amount of information from which to form even a preliminary hiring decision. The hiring authority needs to know, for instance, how many persons constitute "staff' what the applicant's duties as "supervisor" were; the extent of his authority, etc.

— *Continuity*: Has the applicant provided continuity of activity, for instance, in the section detailing earlier employment? Is there an unbroken time line or are there gaps which are unexplained? Often this may be an oversight and can be easily explained. Sometimes such gaps in the time line may be purposeful. For example, applicants who have periods of their life which they feel will be disqualifying in nature simply skip that time-frame and go on to the next. If an applicant had a period of employment from which he was dismissed for cause, he may feel that disclosing such a time or such background will preclude his hiring.

— *Clarify*: If the position in question requires a degree of clear, concise writing skills, has the applicant shown such skills on the application form? Fore example, if the applicant is, for instance, applying for a protection officer position and the duties of that position require on-the-spot, clear and concise report writing, are such skills exhibited on the application form?

Interview Process

During the interview the interviewer has unequalled opportunity to observe the applicant first hand, and view and listen and almost have a sense of what the applicant is about. He can determine certain behavioural patterns such as communication ability, personal grooming standards, ability to listen and apparent ability to understand, alertness, and ability to be at ease. The application form can establish the basis for the formal part of the interview process. The interviewer can, and should, go over each item of the form individually, verifying the applicant's understanding of the query and the completeness of the response. Particular attention should be given to the extent of the applicant's fitness for the job in question—his skills, experience, education and attitude. Related applicant characteristics may also be addressed such as interests, hobbies, and ambitions. The particulars of the job should be previewed. Discuss what the applicant will be expected to do, the hours involved, the tasks, and the environment. Only by a realistic and honest discussion of these factors can an applicant be expected to determine if he is interested.

The Pre-employment Verification (PEV) is an integral and vital part of the employment process, one which can be of tremendous benefit to an employer. When overlooked, it can be tragic. There are lodging managers who feel apprehension about not only doing PEV but about the subject itself in our world of host-related endeavours. Doing a background check on a prospective employee seems to some as bad if not worse than the taboos surrounding our old world security. Not only is this position not defendable, it is counterproductive. When done correctly, there is nothing unethical, unlawful, or immoral about PEV. Lodging managers who, as an excuse not to accomplish PEV, claim that the necessity of hiring an application immediately prohibits pre-employment verification. While the need to hire in an emergency is a dilemma, the answer to the dilemma is obvious.

PEV is a win-win-win situation. Not only does it help a prospective employer to validate job experience, education and qualification, it has a myriad of other advantages. A check of an applicant's criminal history, consistent with the law, may disclose convictions of a type which may cause further inquiry. In a review of an applicant's criminal record might disclose a conviction for forgery some years back and a subsequent sentence which was carried out. Such a record might not be a major consideration if the applicant was applying, for instance, for a chef's position. On the other hand, if the applicant was applying for a position of lifeguard, then multiple convictions for the crime of child molestation would certainly be of interest to the prospective employer.

Methods for Verification Process

The methods of pre-employment verification process include:

— *face-to-face interviews*: This method is often difficult or impracticable to perform. Particularly when the job opening is one which is relatively low on the pay scale and other methods of PEV are possible, this technique usually is not used. If however, the applicant is applying for a higher level position or if references are available from within the existing workforce.

— *telephone checks*: The telephone calls are usually quick and inexpensive. They are also less reliable than other methods. Many properties use a standardised checklist which the caller uses as a reminder to cover all needed and desired subjects.

— *mail correspondence*: *The Use of* mails in PEV is inexpensive and can be useful. It is however quite slow. It is most useful when the information sought is lengthy and statistical in nature and not particularly time-sensitive or subject to interpretation.

— *the use of commercial firms*: These firms, often listed under employment or employee screening will, for a fee, perform the function of pre-employment verification.

Training Programmes

Trained employees are the main resources for the success of any business. Manufacturing firms are virtually assured of failure without trained employees. Retail establishments have failed because they did not have trained employees. Public utilities, financial institutions, health care organisational, without exception, are highly likely to fail unless the personnel responsible for the product or the service which is intended to be delivered to the public are trained.

In all service industries a significant number of employees apply and are employed with little or no previous formal education or training. Even those who arrive with some degree of basic skills are not knowledgeable or informed of the particulars and peculiarities of their new property environment. The training process begins at the time the employee begins his employment and continues until lie leaves that employment is crucial to the success of the property, In literally every department, every manager must accept that fact.

Property success will not evolve unless and until every employee in every department is afforded the process of training in guest protection. Such training is vital because the lodging industry has a high turnover rate. Such training is vital because the lodging industry employs such a high rate of previously untrained persons. Such training is vital because the lodging industry is experiencing, not unlike many other industries, rapid technological changes. The three objectives designed to accomplish the training process are:

— Teach employees to perform new and unfamiliar tasks.

— Assist employees in improving current skills.

— Assure that the guest will be protected.

The elements of training programmes which are useful and necessary to the lodging industry and various types of guest protection training methods are discussed here. The highest level of management on a property has overall training responsibility. In most individual properties, this means the general manager. Often he assigns the responsibility to the human resource department, a unit usually well situated to oversee the plan.

However, the actual conduct of training is often a vastly different concern and thus requires a vastly different approach. Determining needs are the initial consideration of guest protection training—the preparing of a statement of training objectives. Such a statement allows for a common beginning point for all levels of employment from the prospective of management as well as the work force. Guest protection training needs survey. Training needs must initially be determined and this can be accomplished in several ways.

— Determine guest's wants and concerns. There is no surer method of determining guest protection training needs than actually listening to the guest himself. By reading complaint cards, by having the staff listen and report comments received from guests and by successfully utilising guest comment cards, a significant amount of information may be gained.

— Determining what the line employees see as guest protection can be useful. Employees are usually the best source of information. They should be given not only the opportunity to voice their concerns, they should be urged to do so. If an employee sees a guest protection problem, then likely there has been a breakdown in the guest protection training programme.

— Determine the supervisory staff views as actual or potential guest dangers or problems. Usually by soliciting this assistance, department by department, the best results ensue.

— The general manager, during his periodic assessments of the property, should concentrate on those observable items which suggest changes or additions which are needed in the guest protection training programme.

Several methods are used in gleaning this data from several sources. Specifically, the conduit to and through the protection management committee should be fully utilised. Input from all levels of employees, input from guests, and input from vendors and contractors should filter through this committee. Appropriate corrective action then can be accomplished. Individual interviews are also used. This method is often valuable but it is time-consuming and expensive when compared to others. Group interviews allow opportunity in an open atmosphere for employees to make their views known. Questionnaires are used quite frequently.

Organisation and implementation is the another major second step in the development of the guest protection training programme. It involves decisions regarding who will be trained, by whom, where and with what frequency. Training population should be a matter of policy that all employees, in all departments and at all levels will be trained in the specifics of guest protection. This policy should require that guest protection training be mandatory upon initial employment, upon transfer or promotion and on a scheduled basis throughout the career of the employee.

While the overall responsibility for training often lies within the human resource department, specific guest protection training is often best done within individual departments. One reason for this is that the department head is best equipped to manage training time and schedules. Another reason is because guest protection training should be departmentally threat-specific. Those threats which exist in one department may not exist in another and departmental concentration, therefore, for this training is usually advantageous. Still another reason is that the personalities, capabilities, and needs of individual employees are best known to management personnel in their individual departments.

Training methods fall into two categories: group training and individual training. Both have advantages and disadvantages but both should be considered, not only individually but in concert with one another when planning a guest protection training programme.

Group Training

Lecture approach: This approach includes any methods in which presentations before an assembled group are delivered. The lecturer may supplement his presentation with visual aids and often concludes with questions, answers and discussions. This method is often used for guest protection indoctrination training to new property employees. An agenda is set and several managers or departments make prepared presentations. This is the ideal time to introduce the property policy which stresses the absolute requirement that guests be protected at all times in all departments.

Role-playing approach: The approach includes any of several approaches in which a scenario or circumstance is presented to the group and then roles are assigned or taken in order to demonstrate predetermined conclusions. Individuals in the group act, intermittently, as participants and observers and as observers provide feedback to those playing the participative roles. This approach is particularly effective when a trainer has a specific circumstance or setting to be explored. For instance, in a group meeting within the housekeeping department, the executive housekeeper may decide to concentrate on the training of unauthorised access to a guest-room.

The housekeeper may assign one employee from the group the role of the room attendant working in the guest-room hallway and assign to another employee the role of an unknown person who is also found in that hallway. The unknown person can be invited to think of all the reasons he needs to get into a room. The employee playing the role of the room attendant must conjure up appropriate responses to each of the questions. This type approach can be extremely useful not only as a teaching method but in identifying and isolating guest protection subjects about which the employee has questions or is indeed ignorant.

Behaviour modelling: Behaviour modelling takes the approach that repeated behaviour under directed circumstances reinforces that behaviour. This process is geared to specific workplace situations. The training session typically begins with a discussion of the situation to be portrayed and a discussion of the expected learning objective. Behaviour modelling can be adopted into literally any department, often with the department head acting as the role model and performing exactly the behaviour desired, having the employees mimic this behaviour until there is satisfaction that the behaviour is well instilled.

Case study: Members of the group are presented with a guest protection problem, preferably in written form, and are requested to discuss it, analyse it, and come up with solutions.

Individual Training

Individual training methods fall into three categories: on-the-job training, buddy system and coaching.

On-the-job training: This is an essential method of training best described as learning by doing. It is the most common of all lodging training generally and certainly the most common training method in so far as guest protection training is concerned.

Buddy system: It is a true variation of the on-the-job training method and involves a one-on-one approach. An experienced employee who has been at the same property for an extended period of time is assigned to coach a new employee. Perhaps the most common example of the buddy system is that used in the housekeeping department when an experienced room attendant is assigned a new employee to coach.

Coaching: Coaching is designed to address a specific desired change in behaviour. A front desk supervisor who is coaching a trainee can effectively monitor behaviour while that trainee completes the registrations and assigns the appropriate guest-room key. Should the trainee forget and verbalise the room number, the supervisor can take immediate action, recall that key, assign another one correctly and immediately coach the trainee on the desired and necessary behaviour.

14

Role of New Technologies in Hotel Security

Security has always been a key issue for hoteliers. The events of the past seven months have only heightened awareness for proper security and the need for upgrades in equipment, where required. Technology plays a major part in meeting today's security requirements, but there are other important factors in implementing effective security measures.

The people link to technology is critical in the successful use of any security system. The attitude of the hotel staff must be oriented toward security and the proper use of the equipment that is installed. Closed circuit television (CCTV) is not a new platform. The earliest models consisted of a camera fitted with a special lens and connected to a monitor (a television without broadcast reception capability). Systems were later created that added multiple cameras that used switches to rotate the images that were shown on the monitor. The next enhancement came in the form of a video recorder, which captured images on videotape. The original models were reel-to-reel, just like the original audio tape recorders. Later models utilised the same type of video cartridge used by VCRs; in fact, the unit was a modified VCR.

Today's systems include all the above features along with digital colour cameras and images recorded to the hard disk of a personal computer. These images can be retrieved by various criteria and can be archived onto digital audiotape (DAT), CD (RW), DVD or any other digital media. Since retrieval from hard disk is random and not sequential, the time required to review images is greatly reduced. It is important to understand the difference between time-lapse recording and full-motion recording. Time-lapse is actually full motion, but the recording speed is fewer frames per second. The advantage of this technique is a significantly greater length of time can be recorded on either tape or hard drive; however, if the frames per second are set too low a subject could actually pass through an area and not be recorded.

There are many CCTV systems in the marketplace including those from JVC, Panasonic and Sony. Most systems offer high-resolution digital cameras with a motion detector terminal output included. A zoom lever is used to adjust the range of fixed cameras. Other types of cameras feature automatic zoom lens operation. Day and night operations are programmed to detect light levels. Some cameras are infrared sensitive for use in virtual darkness. Digitisation of the signal enhances image quality.

The recording devices use a digital hard drive to store images. Some recorders can store up to 160GB online, with even more capacity available with optional add-on features. An Ethernet network interface device is available for LAN, WAN or Internet connections. This allows monitoring with a conventional Internet browser from any network connection. It is becoming more common for CCTV services to be offered in a package with other applications. Internet-enabled video security is a product offered by StayOnline. The company is a provider of high-speed Internet access for hotels and provides CCTV as part of its services.

The service can use existing cameras and multiplexer by adding a digitiser and installing a video server (PC). The server has an Internet connection that provides recording. The cameras can be monitored from any PC equipped with an Internet connection and a Web browser. This is accomplished by logging on to a secure Web site. This approach offers several benefits including no archiving required on property, providing an alert should cameras be moved or disconnected, and the ability to survey multiple properties from a central location.

TimeLox is now offering a network camera approach along with its most advanced electronic locking system. Integrated with the TimeLox DC-One system, it has the capability for a security officer to hear a doorbell on a computer, view a live picture of the person at the door, and open the door lock from the computer. The system can use either the hotel's local area network or an Internet connection.

The cameras are manufactured by Axis Communications, a worldwide supplier of security and other products. Network cameras have their own IP address and connect directly to a network without using a multiplexer or digitiser. More advanced cameras can detect motion, alarm input/output signals and even send e-mails.

McShane emphasises that no matter what approach is taken for utilising CCTV, proper installation is essential. The correct wiring must be used, cable-TV COAX for older, analog cameras and CAT-5e for more modern, digital cameras. Wiring requirements may vary, however, so the installer must verify the type of wire required with the camera's manufacturer. Training is also a key element to the successful installation of any security equipment. The staff must have an in-depth knowledge of all features and functions. While CCTV is an integral part of hotel security, guestroom locks and safes are equally important. Below is a sampling of some available products.

SAFLOK's Select MT lock offers many attractive features. The lock has the ability to use magnetic stripe, smartcard or memory card technology. The lock itself is a robust one-inch, steel reinforced bead bolt with a three-fourths of an inch latch bolt, creating a double deadbolt effect. An optional automatic deadbolt is also available. SAFLOK will be introducing a wireless lock access network in Chicago. This will convert existing battery-operated locks into online network access control systems. It will also permit two-way communication with the locks for interrogation as well as for the lock communicating that its battery is low.

Security Innovations, Incorporated (SII) specialises in online and real-time access control systems for the lodging industry. SII provides security products that integrate standard electrical and building specifications. VingCard offers two significant products, The DaVinci Locking System and the Elsafe Infinity Series of electronic safes. The contemporary design of these products has bridged the gap between form and function. As an example, the DaVinci series locks come in six different finishes and also offer six different handle designs. This hardware is modular, therefore, offering many different configurations in both appearance and functionality.

One technology that has been proposed for hotels is the use of biometrics to profile guests and identify those that may be involved in some form of criminal activity. These technologies have no place in the hospitality industry. They are intrusive and subject to error, not to mention expensive. McShane suggests better screening of identification will help alleviate these types of concerns. Local security requirements can vary, so address these concerns as well. Security is critical in today's environment, be sure your hotel is not behind.

Safety and Security in Workplace

Safety and Security, like Training and Development, are often left on the back burner until a crisis occurs. By then, people fall victim to crime, get robbed, get assaulted, become sick or even die. Although we mention "safety and security" in one breath, and despite the interrelationship between them, Safety and Security represent two different subjects.

Security encompasses areas such as security of the property itself, company assets, employees' and customers' personal belongings and valuables, life security, personal security, and job security (not covered here because this latter relates to income security), among others. Let us take one "security example" related to employees' personal belongings and valuables in a hotel environment: In all workplaces management stipulates that it is not responsible for valuables and employees personal belongings (their handbags, items kept in the personal lockers, etc.).

Yet management must take all possible measures to prevent theft among employees and of employee belongings through its hiring practices and through the implementation of effective management, human resources and operational policies, such as:

— Background checks of selected applicants

— Policies related to employees' entry to, and exit from, the workplace

— Spot checks of locker rooms and lockers

— Effective supervision and control during the work cycle

— Policies related to the discovery of criminal records and wrongdoing among, and by, employees

— Control of people entering and exiting the workplace

With regard to guest valuables, management informs guests that the hotel is not responsible for valuables left in the room, advising them to secure these in safety deposit boxes provided by the hotel. Besides taking care of security issues related to the people they employee, management must undertake some necessary measures, among which:

— Providing "secure" (safety) deposit boxes and areas to keep valuables
— Policies and practices to ensure the security of these boxes and areas
— Management and operational policies regarding the security of guest rooms
— Management and operational policies regarding the security of public areas
— Security policies and practices for the back-of-the-house areas
— Employment and training of security personnel
— Policies and practices to minimise the "presence" and "patronage" of "shady characters" and criminals, verification of registration and check-in personal data and documentation submitted, and curtailing free movement of unknowns on the premises, as well as direct, free flowing communication with local, national and international security authorities)
— Training of staff in guest and valuable security Effective supervision and control procedures.

When we take the same hotel as example, it is management's duty to ensure "safety" in several areas, such as:

— The structure itself
— Installations and fixtures (check electrical, plumbing, air-conditioning and other installations)

— Public and work areas (e.g. slippery floors, hazardous obstacles in traffic areas), safety of furniture, equipment, appliances, and utensils.

This is followed by:

— Health safety (nontoxic cleaning material and detergents used)

— Good quality air (what we breathe, dependent upon the type of equipment, installations and fixtures used, and regular repairs and maintenance)

— Food safety (a whole world in itself including sanitation, food quality, food spoilage, correct handling procedures, allowable and recommended temperatures, etc.), and checking and control procedures.

An important "preventive measure" is eliminating the possibility of communicating contagious diseases. Even if local regulations do not require it, it is recommended to send food and beverage handlers for regular medical checkup. Another preventive measure is the formulation and implementation of policies and procedures related to employee accidents which may present a threat to food sanitation. Culinary staff who cut themselves accidentally at work, as often happens while slicing food products, have to immediately stop handling food, and report to their Executive Chef and to the person in charge of First Aid in their company for preliminary treatment and handling. Healing and precautionary measures are taken before they are allowed back at their job.

There are also some basic "dress" requirements for staff involved in food and beverage preparations: e.g. Chefs' hats (to prevent hair and whatever hair contains to fall into the food), discreet earrings (non-dangling) or no earrings for women, and long hair neatly and securely tied in a bun at the back of the head. Of no lesser importance is the safety of work tools and work procedures covering all areas, such as stable ladders, secure shelving, safety shoes, well-fitting work garments, clearly written and complete safety procedures and guidelines from management, safety training, and safety installations and equipment, e.g. fire fighting units, regular maintenance schedules for safety equipment and installations, wider traffic areas (to prevent accidents), adequate staffing, and last but not least, continuous effective training in work procedures.

Role of Wireless Technology

From scanners to identify guests upon arrival to remote check-in services, the applications for wireless technology in the hospitality industry seem limitless. At first glance these technologies are a welcome saviour for a more guest-centric experience. Upon closer observation a number of roadblocks impede its progress into the hotel marketplace. While many advances have been made in the industry regarding wireless technology with each advance comes its own list of challenges. When considering a wireless application currently a hotel is faced with a lack of standards across the industry, concern about the payback of the new system and the fact that the current second generation (2G) of wireless applications is sluggish. Dan Phillips said that many of the applications that are being brought into the hospitality industry are technologies that have been developed outside the hotel industry and are being retro-fit to accommodate the needs of hospitality.

When searching for a wireless applications Phillips cautioned that a technology should be brought in to enhance the guest experience and make a hotel more profitable and competitive. Additional challenges to wireless are acceptance of the technology, security of the system and the cost of the new technology. While the security issues can be, and should be, addressed with your perspective provider, the cost issue is one that should be addressed based on the particular application. Antonio Dimilia estimated that a wireless high-speed access system could save up to one-third the cost of rewiring an existing hotel. The non-invasive installation of such a system also can be considered a positive cost advantage as guestrooms would not be taken out of service or guests inconvenienced with an invasive installation.

While some wireless applications cost less than similar traditional solutions other wireless technologies have up front costs with the anticipation of return on investment coming through its administrative use or as a revenue generator over time. According to Dimilia some additional considerations include whether the solution is expandable for future enhancements, does the provider guarantee a level of service and does the provider understand the needs of the guest. Needless to say hoteliers need to carefully consider the vendor's business model to ensure continued support and service 12 months down the road. If the business model doesn't make sense the vendor may not be able to continue its service to your hotel.

A wireless solution currently in action is the MACH-1 (Mobile Access to Carlson Hospitality) system from Carlson Hospitality Worldwide. MACH-1 is completely wireless, running on a Compaq iPAQ system and is used for business information, guest profile information and for management notifications. It is designed to alert management of specific business information, such a VIP at check in or if more than a certain number of guests are waiting for rooms to be cleaned and released or any of a number of triggers defined by management.

Bill Lashley, of Inter-American Data a property management system company servicing large hotels and casinos, believes that the infrastructure for wireless technology is the most important consideration. He mentioned hardware challenges from multiple device communications to a consortium of vendors to develop solutions that continue to need to be overcome. He feels that the technology and cooperation is already ready and available. Inter-American Data has successfully used wireless technology in its Opryland Hotel and The Venetian installations for data collection and check in purposes. He mentioned other practical applications including housekeeping and baggage handling.

Carlson's David Sjolander believes that wireless technology will follow a standard cycle. Based on the Gartner Group hype curve Sjolander charted the emergence of wireless over the following points: technology trigger to the inflated expectations, the trough of disillusionment, the slope of enlightenment, and the plateau of productivity. Following this cycle wireless has already passed through its inflated expectations around the time of BlueTooth hype and is currently working toward the slope of enlightenment, which means that we can expect that there will be a plateau soon where productivity and acceptance of multiple applications will emerge.

Dissatisfaction with Technology

Unquestionably, there is a growing gap between the business needs of the hotel industry and the solutions available to meet those needs. The hotel industry is broadly dissatisfied with the technology available to it, including both the installed base of products and those available as replacements. This dissatisfaction is amplified by the need of many companies to replace aging systems within the next few years due to hardware and software obsolescence. In many cases, support services have been withdrawn by vendors for their oldest legacy products—for entirely understandable reasons, given that some are more than a decade old and run on platforms that are themselves unsupportable.

Most hotel companies face huge capital spending requirements over the next few years to replace legacy systems such as property management systems, telephone switches and software, and central reservations systems. Even for smaller hotel companies, the costs for these replacements can easily total tens of millions of dollars. Yet in most cases, the available replacement systems fail to offer significant business benefit versus the legacy systems they would replace. Features and functionality may be greater, and the technical platform may be newer. But the level of integration with other hotel systems is often worse, and the "newer" technical platform is frequently five or more years behind the current state of the art. Too often, the answer to the question, "why should we spend this money" is not "because it will improve profit" but "because our old system is about to fall apart."

This dissatisfaction is widespread despite the view that there are many technology products on the market that offer more than adequate features and functionality, at least within their defined scopes. Yet with few exceptions, these same products fail to meet the true business needs. Equally, the hotel industry has failed to state those needs to the vendor community clearly, or has stated them in ways that applied only to a subset of the problem.

There are four key reasons for dissatisfaction.

Complexity of Deployment

Most technology products are physically installed at individual hotels but utilise core technologies that are too complex to be supported cost-effectively by hotel staff. Remote management and support of software, either by a corporate technology group or a third party, is often infeasible due to the choice of technologies used to build the software, the lack of understanding of the need by vendors, and the absence of credible third party service providers.

The evolution of products from standalone, turnkey systems into products that operate on the hotel's local area network has created configuration and interoperability issues that neither the vendor nor the hotel staff can easily diagnose or correct. To effectively manage the current generation of technologies in an average full-service hotel, without support from a central technology organisation, can easily require IT skill levels commanding a salary that can rival or exceed that of the general manager.

Obviously, it is neither realistic nor cost-effective for hotels to contemplate this approach. Even among the major management companies and brands that provide centralised support and maintenance of core systems, the requirements of the non-core systems that are purchased and managed locally often overwhelm the capabilities of the on-site IT staff, if indeed there are any. The technical evolution that has created these challenges continues unabated. Absent fundamental change in the systems architecture and delivery model, this situation will continue to get worse.

Inability to Integrate

Hotels have become intense information producers and users, yet still cannot view required information when and where they need it. No common integration method allows the installed systems to work together to effectively create, store, retrieve, and present information that may exist across them.

Proprietary interfaces are seen as expensive and in constant need of upgrade as the respective applications evolve to meet new industry requirements. Furthermore, the growing need for integrated information has resulted in the need for more interfaces and for greater functionality from existing interfaces. The situation has been exacerbated by the need to integrate information not only within the hotel, but at multiple levels of organisations (management company, brand, ownership company, regional cluster). These entities frequently have differing needs and priorities, and competing and incompatible standards.

Standards bodies such as the HITIS and the Open Travel Alliance have focused on a narrow (if critical) range of systems, principally within the distribution chain. While these efforts are important and worthy of strong hotel industry support, the fact remains that very few hotel technology vendors have embraced them and even fewer have implemented them (and in fairness, few of their customers have demanded them). Furthermore, HITIS/ OTA standards address only application- and data-level issues, and not the broader architectural and business issues that often prevent effective system integration.

Role of Hotel Management

Hotel managers cannot, do not want to, and should not be expected to manage complex technology systems. Yet, in the current environment, many are forced to take on this role. Arguably, both the experience of most incumbent general managers, and the success drivers of the business, suggest that general managers should be responsible for filling beds, satisfying guests, and controlling costs. It is naïve to believe that they are capable of making valid purchasing decisions for complex systems, or of managing their technology operation effectively.

This problem is particularly acute for smaller hotel companies, independent hotels, and globally diverse hotel companies, who often lack the financial resources to provide even limited levels of centralised technology management or support.

Unrealised Benefits

Hotel technology investments often fail to deliver the expected benefits. Even when a product meets its functional expectations completely within its intended range, it may prove difficult, costly, or even impossible to integrate it with other components of the hotel's technology. These limitations often become evident only during the implementation of a new system.

The vendor frequently takes the blame when this occurs, but in many cases the limitations may be caused more by the legacy systems than by the replacement. In many cases too, hotel management fails to re-engineer the underlying business processes, and fails to implement the procedures that may be needed to achieve the desired results. Managing this re-engineering process effectively often requires technical project management skills that most hotels cannot find internally – and should not be expected to.

Lack of Strategic Leadership

There is little strategic leadership or vision from either the hotel industry or the vendor community to define the key attributes required of the technology to meet current and future needs, or the key business issues that fund technology investment. While there have been pockets of leadership and vision within the hotel industry and among its technology vendors, too often that leadership and vision has been functionally limited, geographically narrow, market-segment specific, or financially constrained. At other times it delivers functionality but fails to address integration, supportability, or scalability.

Many other industries have the same broad geographic distribution of front-line operations that creates much of the complexity in hospitality. Some of these, such airlines, banks, and retail, are the very industries hotels deal with every day. Yet unlike these industries, the hotel industry lacks any significant presence of major, broad-based product or service vendors with multi-industry expertise to provide technology leadership and vision. Similarly, many hospitality technology executives have worked only within the hotel industry and are unaware of how other industries have addressed some of the same issues they face.

Many hotel companies have been unwilling to fund technology organisations to the level needed to obtain the breadth of experience, creativity, and knowledge of new technologies that is needed to drive change. Finally, technology-related research and development is virtually non-existent within the hotel industry. The result has been incremental rather than generational change, lack of innovation, and persistent reliance on legacy technologies.

Evolution of User Requirements

The historical approach to product development by most hotel technology vendors is no longer relevant. The hotel business is customer-centric, yet much of the available software remains transaction-centric. The transaction-centric model originated in the days when systems were used primarily to deliver a guest folio and to account for the revenue. The industry need has evolved well beyond those requirements. Even some of today's more customer-centric technology offerings often lack the ability to store multiple profiles for the same customer depending on his/her nature of travel. They also fail to recognise the many levels and types of customers (guests, sales accounts, distributors, etc.).

Furthermore, no product or combination of products is capable of delivering a consistent view of the customer across every point of interaction that the customer may have within a single hotel, let alone across multiple hotels within a brand. There are more than 100 categories of technology-based systems in use within the hotel industry, and the average full-service hotel employs at least 20 to 30 different systems. The vast majority of those systems interact with customers in some way or enable service staff to do so. Yet typically only a few (sometimes as few as one) are connected to any system that can accurately describe the customer in even a limited fashion, or record the results of the interaction.

Even where interfaces exist, they may be too expensive to implement, too difficult to maintain, too limited in scope, or simply incapable of delivering the type of customer experience that the hotel wants to provide. Nowhere is this issue more evident than within the distribution process. Hotels want to control how their product is presented to the customer throughout the distribution network, to retain control of the customer relationship, and to customise the experience of the customer based on their knowledge of who the customer is, what they want, and how they behave.

Yet few of the systems within the distribution chain support a notion of "customer" that goes beyond the most basic identifying information. Even where they do, that notion may be lost before delivery of a reservation to the hotel, for lack of an effective interface to the property management system, or even with an interface, for lack of a consistent data model. The evolution of user requirements from transaction-centric to customer-centric is largely unrecognised. Most hotel systems were not designed to be interconnected as fully as today's business needs require and will fall even further short in meeting hotel requirements in the future, creating inefficiencies and opportunities for service-delivery failures. Interfaces that do exist are expensive, difficult to maintain, and often offer only limited functionality.

Impact of Information Infrastructure

Modern technology systems require a consistent and reliable infrastructure, much of which is usually shared among several applications. The key elements of infrastructure are the wide and local area data networks (WANs and LANs), the network operating system, the server and workstation operating systems, and the data management platform. Secondary elements include such items as office automation software, firewalls, virus scanners, and custom reporting packages. These requirements are no different than for businesses in other industries.

Within the hotel industry, however, the required infrastructure is often non-existent. Where it does exist, it is frequently incompatible with modern system requirements. Too often, it is physically crumbling, unsupportable, improperly managed, or vulnerable to security attacks—and quite possibly all at the same time. Different technology products deployed within the same hotel or hotel group not infrequently require infrastructures that are incompatible in critical ways, leading to redundancy, performance degradation, and inability to achieve integration—and all of these can adversely affect guest service and the overall guest experience.

Critical functions such as user authentication, data management, word processing, e-mail, and printer management are often implemented in inconsistent ways, by multiple applications that need to be deployed within the same environment. These functions can and usually are provided by the base operating environment that has been established by the hotel (for example, the combination of Microsoft Windows, Microsoft Office, and Microsoft SQL Server). Their inclusion in end-user applications, with different functionality and unique user interfaces, leads to redundancy, user confusion, and integration challenges.

Some systems even require their own unique, single-use workstations and networks, despite the fact that the intended users may have (or have the need for) standard PCs, connected to the hotel's local area network, to perform other job functions. Some of these problems are legacy-system related, but many result from absence of industry-wide infrastructure standards and ignorance of the impact at the hotel company level.

As an industry, our information assets must be sharable as required across multiple organisations, such as management companies, franchisors, owning companies, suppliers, and distribution partners. Investment in infrastructure that is needed for today's systems may turn out to be totally wasted if the hotel is reflagged or sold tomorrow. It only makes sense to define a common platform that guarantees a minimum level of operability. Yet hotels have not done so to date, and vendor interest in common platforms and interoperability, while growing, is far from sufficient.

Acquisition and Return-on-Investment (ROI) Measurement

More and more aspects of hotel operations and guest room features require integrated technologies, and therefore coordinated acquisition. The existing funding model, typically based on capital acquisition and spread across multiple budgets, creates many obstacles to effective selection and deployment. The diverse and sometimes incompatible needs of owners, managers and franchisors need to be reconciled, and multiple constituencies need to be represented in, and often to sign off on, acquisition decisions. Even individual properties often have multiple owners with conflicting views and priorities.

Vendors cannot easily conclude organisation-wide deals because each organisation has so many competing interests and because each hotel (e.g. within a management company or brand) may need to be "sold" individually. This structure has led many of the largest technology players, who have huge presences across many other industries, to abandon their attempts to establish a significant presence in the hotel industry over frustration with the long sales cycles and the inability to close major, organisation-wide deals.

The capital acquisition model also makes little allowance for technology refresh. Basic items such as workstations, which other industries routinely replace on a regular cycle (such as every three years), are often purchased and left in place until a newly selected system forces their replacement. The cost of those workstations is then factored in as part of the system that requires their replacement, even if other systems use the same workstations (and even if the next upgrade to those other systems will dictate the same workstation upgrade). The extra cost burden may well make the project appear to be financially unviable. Alternatively, the hotel may try to deploy the new system without the recommended upgrade, and then fail to achieve the performance they require. The operational cost of unreliable and inadequate systems is almost invariably ignored.

Hotel budgeting processes recognise the need for physical infrastructure maintenance by creating reserves for furniture, fixtures and equipment (FF&E). This process recognises that the physical infrastructure of the hotel—the lobby, carpeting, and furnishings, for example—requires periodic renovation or replacement, either because it wears out, because customer needs change, or because the asset becomes dated. The very same factors are equally applicable to technology infrastructure, but most hotels treat the replacement or refresh of technology assets as discretionary. Infrastructure projects that are necessary to support future systems are often held to ROI standards, when the benefits are impossible to quantify. Failure to invest over any extended period of time would clearly damage or destroy the hotel's revenue base and limit its ability to adapt to changing business needs, yet the budgeting process treats these investments as discretionary.

One can only imagine what the guest experience might be like if the hotel industry were to hold non-technology infrastructure decisions, such as elevator repair, lobby recarpeting, air conditioning, or roof replacement, to the same ROI standard. Overall, the technology systems and infrastructure are almost never supported in a way commensurate with the fact that they contain the most valuable asset that hotels own – their customer data.

Technical Standards

Many applications in use today are built using aging toolsets and/or are targeted at legacy operating environments. These system environments were at one time relevant, and provided a low-cost base from which to deliver increased functionality. In today's modern, networked and Internet-connected world, however, these systems do not provide the needed connectivity to, or integration with, the many other applications that hotels are required to operate.

For a variety of valid business reasons, hotels need to interconnect complementary products produced by vendors who may be direct competitors, either in the same or in other application areas. Yet these interconnections are often frustrated by architectural in-compatibilities.

Many application vendors, for example, are still in the process of migrating MS-DOS based applications to Windows, at a time when technology has moved through several generations of Windows and is now shifting to the Web. Given the multi-vendor landscape of the industry, a new approach is needed, one based on the effective use of available, modern technologies, and that allows rapid feature function development and facilitates easier application integration, deployment, management and upgrade.

Progress toward any technical standard will be evolutionary, and vendors cannot be expected to convert their legacy systems to meet new standards over-night. These standards are not intended to be flexible, but rather the application of the standards in hotel purchasing decisions will of necessity be flexible, at least in the short term. The desired result can be achieved if technology buyers make their commitment to long-term achievement of the standards a critical element of the evaluation, negotiation, and contracting process.

Business Standards

Many of the limitations of the current situation have evolved from contractual restrictions in software licensing and usage, and in the limited willingness or ability of many technology vendors to support the integration requirements of their hotel customers. While the technical standards create the platform for open systems, business standards are needed to ensure that hotel companies have the contractual right to license and integrate systems as needed, even where competing vendors are involved, and using whatever means of integration are available and appropriate. At the same times, vendors have the right to protect their intellectual property, and to compete in the provision of software and services that assist in or accomplish such integration.

We urge vendors and hotels to adopt these forward-thinking business standards that are responsive to hotel industry needs.

1. Vendors who do (or who wish to) offer complementary products to common customer base are encouraged to work together in open and effective partnerships, to make common choices with regard to infrastructure and architecture, and to provide a cohesive set of interoperable software and related delivery and support services. This approach will reduce the total cost of ownership to hotels significantly, improve the vendors' ability to deliver the solution the hotels need, reduce support costs for the vendors, and therefore be expected to increase the sales and profitability of the participating vendors.
2. Vendors should agree to provide open-systems access to their technologies. Vendors are encouraged to provide comprehensive, real-time, transaction-based interfaces, and hotels are encouraged to utilise vendor-provided interfaces. However, if a hotel concludes that a vendor cannot provide the appropriate interface in a cost-effective manner, the software license or use contract should not restrict the hotel from acquiring a third-party interface or from building its own. Software should include comprehensive documentation of data structures, procedure calls, security, and other functionality that another party may reasonably require in order to effect interoperability for a hotel. In the absence of comprehensive documentation, or in the event of unclear documentation, vendors should be contractually required to assist third parties to the degree needed for the third party to complete its tasks. Vendors should not be expected to provide their competitors with details regarding the means by which their code accomplishes specific tasks internally,

nor should they be expected to provide documentation to parties that do not have a bona fide need based on an actual customer.

3. Vendors should not impose contractual restrictions that would prevent a hotel from contracting any third party of the hotel's choosing to develop integration capabilities to the vendors' software, such as restrictions on who may have access to documentation or to live systems. Vendors should be entitled to notice from the hotel company when a third-party integration requires such documentation or access, and should be able to impose reasonable restrictions on the scope, extent, and duration of access and on the rights of the third party to retain copies of documentation, provided that those restrictions do not prevent the third party from effectively achieving their objectives.
4. Hotels should agree to honour the intellectual property rights of vendors' products and to enforce the vendors' rights with respect to any sub-contractors who have access to the vendors' system.
5. Vendor consortia that claim interoperability of their respective applications (including by traditional interfaces) should individually and collectively commit to technical support and performance service levels on an end-to-end basis. Such cooperating vendors should implement a single point of contact support for integration issues, with defined escalation processes within each vendor's support and development organisations. This approach should not only improve end-user support but, properly implemented, will reduce vendors' support costs.
6. Contracts should clearly state that data entered into, created by or inherited by any technology system is owned by the hotel as customer. The hotel should have the right, and be provided with the means, to

extract its data in a usable format. Vendors have no rights to use the hotel's data except for (a) rights specifically granted by the hotel; and (b) the right to use aggregate customer production metrics (across all of its customers combined) as indications of vendor's industry volume. Exception (b) should not apply to any customer or group of related customers that constitutes more than one-third of the vendor's total volume on a particular metric.

7. Hotels should strongly consider the benefits of working with vendors who adhere to the standards and should seek to recognise, patronise, and endorse them for their commitment to improving the industry's technical capabilities.

Policies and Practice of Hotel Industry

Many of the challenges in the hotel technology arena have been created by policies and practices of hotel companies themselves. In order to achieve success, a substantial number of hotel companies may need to change key elements of how they measure, fund, and purchase technology. In some cases these changes can be effected through the auspices of trade organisations such as HFTP; while in other instances they must be undertaken by each hotel company independently. Many of these actions are outside the CIO's scope of responsibility, and will require the endorsement and adoption by hotel company CEOs, COOs, CFOs, and Boards of Directors.

Improve Technology Cost Measurement

The consultants among the founding members of HTNG are continually asked by major industry players to assist in developing solid estimates of industry technology spending. Despite the level of interest among CEOs and CIOs within the industry, technology cost measurement has proven extremely elusive. There is a widespread view among many companies that, while service delivery models for technology (ASP services being one example) are attractive, the current offerings on the marketplace seem too expensive in comparison to acquisition costs.

While this may be true in some cases, there are fundamental issues with attempts to compare service models with capital spending models. First, current hotel accounting standards make it virtually impossible to measure technology costs. Most technology costs within the hotel are buried within departmental budgets. Costs for a single technology initiative typically span across departmental borders. Technology that is provisioned by management companies or franchisors is often priced to the hotels at an amount that bears at best a loose relationship to underlying costs (and sometimes no relationship at all).

Second, many of the costs borne within the service model are typically excluded when estimating the total cost of ownership of an alternative capital-acquisition based solution. Internal cost calculations rarely include the time of all of the IT and non-IT management and staff needed to manage the operation on an ongoing basis. Furthermore, hotel companies rarely hold internal service departments to the same service-level agreements that they insist upon with external service providers.

Perhaps even more important, the service model typically includes regular technology refresh that would lead to additional downline costs in the capital acquisition model, most (or all) of which are often not considered. One of the consultants in our group has estimated that these issues can cause the typical capital acquisition funding approach to under-state true costs by 30% or more. The industry as a whole needs to find a better way to capture technology costs within its accounting systems. This role should logically fall within the scope of HFTP's charter. In order to manage technology spending appropriately, the hotel industry's accounting, budgeting and ROI analysis approaches need to:

— Clearly identify technology costs by category (e.g. infrastructure, operational systems, sales/marketing/ distribution, guest room, etc.), regardless of which department funds them.

— Clearly measure or, at a minimum, estimate, indirect costs of technology projects, including management staff time, burdens on support departments such as accounting and human resources, and similar resources.

— Measure technology costs actually incurred by the hotel, management company, and franchisor levels, and paid to third-party (unrelated) vendors. Too often, technology projects are mis-analysed and underfunded because a manager or franchisor imposes a cost on a hotel that covers the provision of both technology-based and non-technology services. The hotel experiences a single price for the service and may not be able to assess the technology components independently.

— Make explicit assumptions about technology refresh costs, and in particular about the organisational costs when change is generational (as is often the case with the capital acquisition model) vs. incremental (as is more common with the service model).

— Identify costs shared among multiple applications as infrastructure, and evaluate infrastructure costs within the context of all supported applications and operations rather than just the single application that forced an upgrade or replacement

Reserve Funds for Technology

Hotels should establish, and owners should demand,

explicit technology reserves, just as they create reserves to refurbish the hotel's physical plant. The need to spend money on an ongoing basis to ensure a stable but evolving technology environment is not optional, but rather is a cost of staying in business. While it may be possible to defer a given expenditure from one year to the next, technology refresh cannot be put off forever any more than can refurbishment of the physical plant.

Measured Infrastructure Costs

The need to measure shared infrastructure costs, discussed above, is generated by the need to budget for it separately from end-user projects. A solid technology foundation within each hotel and hotel company is required to operate any of the more modern hotel systems. Today, the property management system, the sales system, the local presence of the central reservation system, the office automation software, and many other applications often share the network infrastructure and workstations, which taken together can account for half or more of the hardware costs within a hotel. In the future, PABXs, telephone handsets, in-room entertainment and Internet services, door locking, and energy control systems (among others) will likely share the same infrastructure.

The cost of maintaining reasonably current technology for the shared infrastructure elements cannot reasonably be burdened on any one application and justified by the project's ROI. Rather, infrastructure costs should be determined, component by component, with reasonable lifetimes, and an annual budget established for technology refresh. The particular systems being deployed or upgraded within a given budget year may dictate which infrastructure elements are refreshed first, but should not be expected to provide the financial justification for infrastructure elements that would eventually be needed with or without the project.

An example of this approach is the widespread use in other industries (and in isolated pockets within the hotel industry) of leasing models for technology infrastructure. Many companies, for example, routinely replace all PCs on a three-year cycle. The vendor that provisions the PCs (whether internal or external) charges the users a monthly lease rate that enables it to deliver, install, maintain, and replace PCs. This maintenance and replacement cycle allows every technology project to assume that it has the workstations needed, at a current level of technology. The incremental cost of the project is affected only if it creates the need for additional workstations.

Vendors in Hotel Technology

Vendors within the hotel technology community each have their own business models and agendas. Ultimately, however, the hotels are their customers, and those vendors who listen to hotels and who provide technology that hotels can use more effectively, will prosper along with their clients. Hotel companies should talk with their current vendors and determine their willingness to commit to the standards. If vendors understand that their future business from enough hotel companies is dependent on their operating within a standard technical and business framework, most of them will adapt very quickly. There are no requirements imposed by these standards that have not been widely adopted by the technology communities in other industries. Individual vendors may balk, but at the end of the day, it is the hotel's money to spend with the vendors who can best serve their needs.

Recruitment of IT Professionals

The hotel industry as a whole, and individual hotel properties in particular, have failed to embrace the establishment of adequately funded and qualified technical staff. While there are many structural reasons why hotel technology has failed to deliver to its potential, many could have been avoided, or could be compensated for, if an adequate IT skill base were available. Only a few hotel companies, mostly larger ones, have embraced this concept. As an industry, we would not promote an accountant or front desk clerk to the top position in food and beverage, yet hotels routinely promote unqualified staff into key technology positions. If the food is bad and the restaurant service surly, we find a qualified F&B manager and give him or her what is needed to succeed.

When technology fails to deliver to expectation, we find the staff member who seems to know how to use a computer and ask them to solve it. This is akin to selecting, for the next F&B manager or Executive Chef, someone who likes to eat. For many hotels, and particularly those lacking centralised support from a chain or management company, hiring qualified IT staff can be an immense challenge. An IT professional sufficiently skilled to manage all of the technology in a midsized or large hotel can command a salary equal to or greater than that of the General Manager.

Realistically, a 500-room hotel can easily have US$2 million to $4 million in technology costs, which we as an industry have often entrusted to $40,000-a-year staff who can, at best, be expected to have minimal experience in a very limited set of technical fields. There are dozens of technical disciplines required to manage technology in a hotel, and an IT person at such a salary level is unlikely to even be aware of many of them, much less competent to manage them. Larger management companies, chains, and third-party service providers are inherently in a better position to attract qualified staff with the necessary range of expertise. It is for this reason that most larger companies and some service vendors have begun pulling technology out of hotels, wherever feasible, operating it in a centralised or regionalised environment, and delivering it as a service to hotels. This is not to say that hotels do not need their own IT staff, or to suggest that it would allow hotels to continue to get by with the current insufficient levels of IT skills. Rather, it will allow a competent IT manager within a hotel to deliver and support a broad range of technology services cost effectively.

As an industry, we need to upgrade the position of IT manager, in all but the most basic types of hotels, to an executive committee level position, with commensurate pay, so that we can hire IT professionals with the qualifications needed to run the diverse systems we use. Perhaps in the future, if the industry evolves to more standard software delivered by third-parties and management companies, this position can be eliminated, but for the next five to ten years it is likely to be essential for most hotels. When we hire IT professionals, whether at the corporate or hotel level, we should be looking at their range of technical education and skillsets more than their hotel experience. We need more IT people at all levels who know how problems have been solved in other industries and disciplines, and who have been trained to solve these problems in a professional way. We can teach them what they need to know about hotels; we cannot as an industry teach them what they need to know about technology.

Future Challenges of Technology in the Hotel Industry

Hotel technology vendors are mostly small and undercapitalised. While there is much in the way of quality product to meet each area of functional need, each product addresses only a very limited set of the total application requirements. Interoperability of systems, with a few notable exceptions, has been an elusive goal. Annual global hotel technology spending has been estimated by various studies to be as high as US$25 billion, although the truth is that, as technology expenses are buried in so many parts of hotel budgets, such estimates are at best educated guesses. By any measure, however, hospitality represents one of the largest industries in terms of technology spend, perhaps surpassed only by the retail industry and the technology industry itself.

The largest software providers and technology service delivery companies in the hotel industry each command less than 1% of the market. The vast majority of vendors have market shares of less than 0.1%. Many major software and service providers that dominate other industries have left this huge market largely untouched. Others recognised the opportunity and tried to stake out positions, but have been largely unsuccessful. Several have abandoned the industry completely, often after years of frustration and losses.

Among the existing set of hotel technology vendors, only a few have achieved any significant success with consolidation or partnership strategies, whether by acquisition, through alliances, or through internal development. Even these more successful companies, however, have barely achieved 1% market shares. The resulting fragmentation of systems and vendors has imposed significant costs and inefficiencies on hotels. At the property level, it requires high levels of management effort to manage the multi-system, multi-vendor environment.

For multi-hotel organisations (whether management, ownership, franchise, or membership), it complicates the consolidation of accurate, comprehensive data on guests' profiles, preferences and activities—the lifeblood of any hospitality organisation. Similarly, the industry structure has imposed costs on technology vendors. The frequent need for capital budget approval of multiple parties just to sell to a single hotel (much less a multi-hotel organisation) have led to high selling costs, long sales cycles, and lagging financial performance among vendors. Access to seed capital has been limited, and exit strategies have proven difficult to execute.

Twenty-five years ago, for example, the U.S. banking industry was highly fragmented and dominated by small, independent branch banks. Technology had become critical to competitive success, yet the software and service suppliers to the industry were nearly as fragmented as in the hotel industry today. Branch managers and holding company executives in the banking industry in the 1970s and 1980s voiced many of the same concerns raised today by hotel general managers and executives.

Yet today, the vast majority of U.S. branch banks receive all of their technology, delivered to them as a service by one of three independent commercial vendors. It is only because of this structure that the technology suppliers to the banking industry have been able to deliver a reasonably customer-centric, consistent technology ... one that facilitates the financial side of world trade, enables customers to use their ATM cards around the world, allows banks to cross-sell a range of financial products, and frees bank managers to focus on customer retention and profitability rather than technology.

Like the hotel industry, the retail industry is dominated by small outlets with mixed ownership, management, and franchise relationships. Yet retail has achieved quite a high degree of supply chain integration, point-of-sale consistency across a wide variety of merchants, and merchandise management strategies. Those accomplishments would have been impossible without the emergence of technology standards, vendors who supported them, and products that were interoperable even, when required, with competitive systems.

Without these developments, credit cards would only work if the cardholder's issuing bank was the same as the merchant's, and ATM cards would only work with the issuing bank's own cash machines. In each case, the emergence of single-source, full-solution vendors, who can offer turnkey technology on a pay-as-you-go basis, frees the business unit to focus on meeting the needs of its customers, without having to worry about managing complex technology.

— These single-source vendors can focus on ease of use and simplicity of management for the end user.

— In many cases the underlying applications may consist of a patchwork of legacy solutions and newer technologies, but the end user sees a single, consistent, evolving application.

— Software upgrades occur seamlessly, the equipment and networks are reliable, and the applications are nearly bug-free.

— Application suites meet nearly every need of the business unit, and can be configured to meet the competitive requirements of widely varying strategies.

— The cost to the business unit is known in advance and can be budgeted as an operating expense, often directly tied to revenue-generating transactions.

— Over time, the vendors can reduce operating and maintenance costs by rewriting legacy applications into a consistent, modern technology platform.

Simply put, today's branch bank or retail store manager worries no more about technology than he or she worries about the electricity, water supply, or telephone. They pay the "utility" bill each month, and the technology arrives. In the rare instances where it fails, they call the "utility" company and have it repaired.

Discrimination and Retaliation Claims

Employers making lay-offs should expect discrimination, harassment and retaliation claims. Some employees may claim that they are being singled out because of past issues involving harassment or discrimination or because they are being "targeted" for the lay-off or termination based on age, race, national origin, religion, disability, gender or any number of other "protected categories" under the law.

Unfortunately, it is not a complete defence for the employer to argue that "business necessity" required the adverse action. For example, in a claim involving retaliation, the employer will have to demonstrate that it properly dealt with the discrimination or harassment claim originally and that such claim had no causal connection with the decision to lay-off or terminate the individual later. Similarly, in a discrimination claim involving the allegation that certain employees in a protected category are "targeted," the employer will have to demonstrate that there are solid business reasons for choosing one employee or group of employees over others.

To minimise claims of this nature, employers should have enforceable arbitration programmes in place that comply with recent Supreme Court guidelines for enforceability. Also, employers should analyse all lay-off or reorganisation decisions with counsel to ensure that no workers in protected categories — such as individuals over 40 — are disproportionately affected by the adverse employment action. Personnel files should be reviewed to flag possible issues involving past claims of harassment or discrimination that could lead to retaliation claims.

Labour Problems

Hospitality industry employers with unionised work forces have additional contractual and legal obligations which affect the employer's right to eliminate jobs. Most labour agreements contain lay-off clauses which typically obligate the employer to paying severance, benefits and, in some instances, early retirement incentives. Lay-off clauses may also restrict both the elimination of certain jobs and the number of employees that may be laid off. In some instances, they may mandate that the employer follow a specified order in the lay-offs. During effects bargaining, unions often make additional demands regarding the payout of severance and benefits and the application of seniority with respect to lay-offs.

Typically, unions will demand that seniority — not qualifications or competency — be the determining factor in lay-offs. This may not be in the best interest of an employer who wants to maintain the highest level of customer service while streamlining its operations. Where the employer has cash flow problems, it may be difficult to pay hefty severance packages. Some labour agreements contain "force majeure" or other emergency clauses which employers may invoke, under the right circumstances, to circumvent onerous contractual obligations. Indeed, several air carriers denied furloughed airline workers severance pay and other lay-off benefits when the airlines invoked force majeure clauses immediately after September 11.

Hospitality employers faced with the prospect of reducing a unionised workforce should consider the cost and operational implications triggered by adherence to union demands or contractual obligations. Alternatives, such as loopholes in the collective bargaining agreement or the possible renegotiation, mid-term, of certain contract provisions should be considered.

Employers are subject to state and federal laws regulating the payment of final wages and other benefits upon an employee's termination, even where there are no WARN Act or union obligations. The general rule is that employees who are discharged or laid off must be paid on the last day of work for all wages earned, including accrued vacation, through the end of their employment. In addition to accrued vacation, employers must pay terminated employees in cash for any accrued time off if set forth in a policy, whether the time-off was accrued under a paid time-off policy or by agreement to receive compensatory time-off in lieu of overtime hours worked.

"Wages" that must be paid upon termination may also include commission and bonus arrangements that were entered into with employees during more economically healthy times. While an employer's failure to pay wages promptly to a terminated employee may result in waiting time penalties, in addition to the monies owed, there are certain circumstances in which employers may be able to forestall or avoid paying other types of compensation, such as commissions or bonuses. For example, depending on how the commission or bonus arrangement was structured with the employee, the employer may have a contractual defence that no commission was owed at all at the time of the employee's termination.

Employers should review existing commission and bonus arrangements to determine their applicability to certain business risks and uncertainty. Once decisions are made with respect to employment terminations, it may be too late to rearrange commission or bonus structures. Before these decisions are made is the time for employers to review commission, bonus plans, vacation and other benefit policies, to redefine them in a manner more employer-sensitive to adverse economic conditions.

One often overlooked area of law applicable to employee lay-offs is the employer's obligation to provide the opportunity for continuing health coverage to terminated employees. When an employer provides medical coverage to its employees, and it does so pursuant to the terms of a benefit plan sponsored and administered by the employer, the plan will be subject to regulation under ERISA. Such requirements usually include continuation coverage rights to employees and their dependents under COBRA. On the other hand, if the employer is going out of business or has been acquired by a successor, the COBRA obligation may be eliminated or passed on to a successor employer.

Employers often wonder if lay-off decisions can affect employees who are on a leave of absence. For example, can employers institute job eliminations or reductions that will result in the termination of employees who are out on pregnancy leave, disability leave, workers' compensation leave or family and medical leave? The answer will typically depend on a variety of factors, but most significantly the business reasons for the lay-off and whether the lay-off evenly affects both active employees as well as employees on a leave of absence.

To minimise the risk of retaliation claims by employees on a leave of absence whose positions are eliminated, employers must properly document the business reasons supporting the lay-off decisions and consult with labour counsel to consider the risks involved in such decisions.

BIBLIOGRAPHY

Barrett E.B, Penner K.P., *Food safety checklist for foodservice operations*, Cooperative Extension Service, Manhattan, KS, 1995.

Bryant T, Barrett B., "Determining the food safety and handwashing practices of 4th, 5th, and 6th graders", *Journal of the American Dietetic Association*, 100(9), A-68, 2000.

Lattin, Gerald W., *Lodging and Food Service Industry*, East Lansing: Educational Institute of the American Hotel & Motel Association, 1995.

Lewis, Robert C., *Cases in Hospitality Marketing and Management*, New York: John Wiley, 1997.

Loken, Joan K., *The HACCP Food Safety Manual*, New York: Wiley, 1995.

Lucas, Rosemary E., *Managing Employee Relations in the Hotel and Catering Industry*, London: Cassell, 1995.

McSwane, David Zachary, *Essentials of Food Safety and Sanitation*, Upper Saddle River: Prentice Hall, 2000.

Ninemeier, Jack D., *Management of Food and Beverage Operations*, East Lansing: Educational Institute of the American Hotel and Motel Association, 1995.

Professional Chef's Techniques of Healthy Cooking, New York: John Wiley & Sons, 1993.

Rande, Wallace L. *Introduction to Professional Foodservice*, New York: Wiley, 1996.

Reed, Lewis. *Specs: The Comprehensive Foodservice Purchasing and Specification Manual*, Van Nostrand Reinhold, 1993.

Riedel, R. A., *Hotel Air Quality Management: An Action Guide for Managers and Engineers*, East Lansing: Educational Institute of the American Hotel & Motel Association, 1995.

Riley, Michael, *Managing People: A Guide for Managers in the Hotel and Catering Industry*, Oxford: Butterworth Heinemann, 1995.

Ruhlman, Michael, *The Making of a Chef: Mastering Heat at the Culinary Institute of America*, New York: Henry Holt, 1997.

INDEX